"Sheri Rose Shepherd reminds us that pride, guilt, procrastination, greed, and other sins of the flesh keep us from living out our purpose—but true crowning moments occur when we fix our eyes on eternity. Her message will challenge readers to prepare to meet the Prince of Peace by focusing on the things that matter most."

JAMES AND BETTY ROBISON
LIFE OUTREACH INTERNATIONAL
FORT WORTH, TEXAS

"This a timely, timeless, and empowering word for all princesses in waiting. Jesus is truly coming back for a Bride, and we are admonished to make ourselves ready. *My Prince Will Come* is just such an adornment for the daughters. It will cover shame with beauty, hopelessness with vision, and restore strength to every weak and broken place. Let the beauty of this book wash over you."

LISA BEVERE
SPEAKER AND BESTSELLING AUTHOR OF
KISSED THE GIRLS AND MADE THEM CRY

My Prince Will Come

Sheri Rose SHEPHERD

Multnomah® Publishers *Sisters, Oregon*

MY PRINCE WILL COME
© 2005 by Sheri Rose Shepherd

published by Multnomah® Publishers, Inc.
International Standard Book Number: 1-59052-531-0

Cover design by DesignWorksGroup, Inc.
Cover image by John Lund/Getty Images

Scripture quotations are taken from:
The Living Bible (TLB) © 1971. Used by permission of Tyndale House Publishers, Inc. All rights reserved.
The Holy Bible, New International Version (NIV)© 1973, 1984 by International Bible Society,
used by permission of Zondervan Publishing House
The Holy Bible, New International Reader's Version. Copyright © 1994, 1996 by International Bible Society.
Used by permission of Zondervan Publishing House. All rights reserved.
Contemporary English Version (CEV) © 1995 by American Bible Society
The Amplified Bible (AMP) © 1965, 1987 by Zondervan Publishing House.
The Message by Eugene H. Peterson, Copyright " 1993, 1994, 1995, 1996, 2000.
Used by permission of NavPress Publishing Group. All rights reserved.
Holy Bible, New Living Translation (NLT) © 1996. Used by permission of
Tyndale House Publishers, Inc. All rights reserved.
The Holy Bible, New King James Version (NKJV) © 1984 by Thomas Nelson, Inc.
New American Standard Bible (NASB) © 1960, 1977 by the Lockman Foundation
The Holy Bible, English Standard Version (ESV) © 2001 by Crossway Bibles, a division of Good News
Publishers. Used by permission. All rights reserved.

Multnomah is a trademark of Multnomah Publishers, Inc.,
and is registered in the U.S. Patent and Trademark Office.
The colophon is a trademark of Multnomah Publishers, Inc.

Printed in China

For information:
MULTNOMAH PUBLISHERS, INC. · 601 N. LARCH ST. · SISTERS, OR 97759

Library of Congress Cataloging-in-Publication Data

Shepherd, Sheri Rose, 1961-
  My prince will come : getting ready for my Lord's return / by Sheri Rose Shepherd.
    p. cm.
  ISBN 1-59052-531-0
  1. Second Advent. I. Title.
BT886.3.S58 2005
236′.9—dc22

2005012897

05 06 07 08 09 10 11 12—10 9 8 7 6 5 4 3 2 1 0

Contents

Our Prince Will Come...

*And I...saw the Holy City, the new Jerusalem,
coming down from God out of heaven.
It was a glorious sight, beautiful as a bride at her wedding.*

REVELATION 21:2, TLB

he bride-to-be stood motionless, staring in the mirror for what seemed like an eternity. She had worked hard to prepare for this moment. Her hair and makeup were works of art, and her dress was stunning. Never before had she felt so perfectly beautiful. But something was *still* missing. Something had gone terribly wrong.

Where were her bridesmaids? Where were her guests? Had she not made it clear to everyone that this day was coming? The most glorious day of all time? She glanced over at the open guest book beside her—blank. The gift table—empty…except for a stack of unopened letters. Were those the wedding invitations she should have sent out? No, they couldn't be. She was sure she had mailed them weeks ago and crossed that item off her list.

The bride fumbled through the pile. Every letter was addressed to her, and each had been sent from the same person—her Betrothed. Of course she recognized His handwriting. She had read His letters before—long ago— but life had kept her so busy that there really hadn't been any time to read His letters. *There will be plenty of time to get to know my husband after the wedding*, she had thought.

The bride sifted through the pile, looking for something without really knowing what. Tears of disappointment blurred her vision, but she stopped at a particular letter. Her eyes brightened as she read the familiar phrase her Prince had written on the envelope: *"I can't wait to see you, My dearest princess! I love you!"* A sense of eagerness overcame her, and she began to open the envelope. But just then she heard the sound of the most beautiful music she had ever heard. The wedding march had begun! She dropped the letter and ran toward the large double doors that opened into the sanctuary. She could fill the sweet presence of her Prince in the empty hall. Where were her friends? Her family? Hadn't they gotten their invitations? Maybe they were too busy to come? She wrestled with these unanswered questions as she slowly walked down the aisle of the large and gloriously decorated sanctuary. Her eyes danced about as she absorbed the indescribable beauty of her surroundings. Then, suddenly, everything around her seemed to blur as she caught sight of Him.

He looked so tender and loving standing there at the end of the aisle, patiently waiting for His bride to approach. There were no bridesmaids or groomsmen, only her Groom and what appeared to be stacks and stacks of wedding presents. She had heard that her Prince had prepared many gifts for His bride, but this was truly overwhelming.

She always knew her emotions would run wild on her wedding day, but nothing had prepared her for the intense flood that filled and overflowed her heart. As she approached her Groom—her Prince—she felt her heart race and her face flush with shame and embarrassment. It hit her suddenly like a stabbing jolt of reality: He had done everything to prepare this day for her. He had done everything to woo her, to bless her, to capture her heart, to rescue her…and she had done nothing! She had nothing to offer Him. No gifts. No guests. She had labored and sweated over all the wrong things and for all the wrong reasons. The depth of her shame was so intense that she grabbed the hem of her gown and turned, ready to run away. It was then that her eyes met His.

There she saw something in His gaze that was more intense than her shame, more powerful than her guilt. That "something" was greater than anything she had ever felt before. She turned back toward Him and slowly continued down the aisle. Then it happened. Not all at once, but gradually. As she walked…as she approached her Prince…as she stared into His tender eyes…her shame began to melt away. Closer. Closer still. Now she could see it: The look on His face was one of pure love, the kind of love that says, "You are Mine, My princess, and nothing can keep us apart."

As the bride-to-be stepped up to stand next to her Groom, every negative emotion loosed its grip on her and departed forever. Every pain that had burrowed its way into her soul disappeared for good. The Prince extended His hand and took hers. As they stood there face-to-face, she realized that her life was finally complete and her joy more full than she had ever dreamed possible. The Prince smiled and gently wiped away the tears from her cheek. He then embraced His new bride and said, "You will never cry again, My love. Welcome home."

If you know Jesus as your Savior, then He is your Prince, you are His princess, and this story is about your glorious day. However, the end of this story and the fruits of that day are, to some degree, up to you, His bride-to-be. By God's grace, will you be ready to meet Him face-to-face on that majestic day of His return? Are you ready for your Prince? Does the way you live your life today reflect that you are His? Do you need to take the time to fall in love once again with the One who gave His life for you? Are you ready to discover your "happily ever after"? Do you need Him to reveal Himself to you in a very real and personal way? Is it your heart's desire to live a passionate, Christ-centered life? Do you need Him to set you free to live in the complete freedom He has already won for you?

If your answer to any or all of the above questions is yes, then I invite you to take a seat and read about the greatest love story ever told—written for *you*—and discover how you can prepare yourself for your Prince!

Love,

Your sister princess in Christ,

Sheri Rose

> "*No eye has seen, no ear has heard,
> and no mind has imagined
> what God has prepared
> for those who love Him.*"
>
> 1 CORINTHIANS 2:9, NLT

one

The Crowning Moment

TAKING YOUR ROYAL POSITION

he lights were shining brightly in my eyes. My heart was racing as I stood there staring out at an audience of strangers who were anxiously watching to see who would win the crown. Among those two thousand strangers in the audience were my precious family members and friends who knew how much God had enabled me to overcome in my life and what a miracle my standing on that stage was.

As I waited for the big announcement, I began to think, *Is this really what I need and want—to win a worldly crown?* As the envelope that held the winner's name was passed to the master of ceremonies, I glanced at the panel of judges. *Am I placing my sense of worth in the hands of these people's evaluation*

of me? Then my eyes moved to the other women competing for the same crown. Each of them must have a story to tell and something to share with the world if she should be crowned. Somehow it did not seem right that only one of us would be chosen. Each of us longed to have that crown placed on our heads, something symbolic to make us special. At last, the crowning moment arrived.

The countdown began with the fourth runner-up. My stomach was in knots as the master of ceremonies slowly announced the judges' decisions. Each of us left standing on stage after a runner-up was named felt a trembling hope of winning and an impossible-to-ignore fear of rejection.

Then it happened—my crowning moment, the moment of affirmation I had dreamed about most of my life! The master of ceremonies called my name as the 1994 Mrs. United States of America. Overwhelmed with joy, I cried as that worldly crown was placed on my head and the crystal-beaded banner was hung over my shoulder. Cameras flashed, people applauded, and women gathered around me to celebrate my victory. It was one of those moments in life that words could never truly describe.

But when the cameras stopped flashing, the audience emptied out of the auditorium, and the celebration came to an end, I walked back to my hotel room. I took off the crown and laid it on the table by the window. I turned off the lights and noticed that the crystal crown sparkled with the reflection of the full moon and the bright Las Vegas lights.

As I stared at the beautiful crown that I had so longed for, I began to think about my Lord. I remembered the night when, in my darkest hour, He had crowned me with His tender love and mercy. It had happened ten years earlier in a different hotel room. I had felt hopeless and desperate for someone or something to fill my empty soul.

At that time in my life, I had all the things that should have meant happiness and fulfillment. I was no longer addicted to drugs, I had lost sixty pounds, and I owned my own business. I had money, success, beauty titles, boyfriends, nice clothes, and people's approval for all I had overcome. I drove a nice car and had a calendar full of appointments for places to go and people to see. Yet I still cried myself to sleep at night and battled depression as well as an eating disorder called bulimia. On the outside I looked like I had it all together, but on the inside I was falling apart. I felt empty and alone even when I was in a crowd of people. I could not find anything or anyone to fill that deep lonely place in my heart. I wanted to die.

Feeling as if I had nothing to live for and deciding that I could not go on any longer, I checked into a hotel room. My plan was to end my life with an overdose of sleeping pills. Yet at that moment, my most desperate moment, I cried out to God. He was my last hope—He heard my cry and rescued me before I took my life. At that moment in the hotel room, I actually felt God's holy presence with me, and for the first time in my life, I did not feel alone. Instead I felt loved and at peace.

Our God promises that if we will seek Him with all our heart, we *will* find Him. I discovered the truth of that promise. When I called out to God that night, He gave me the greatest crown of all. It was not a crown bestowed by man, but the crown of life—of everlasting life—bestowed by God. He restored my soul and gave me everything that I had been desperately searching for: love, joy, peace of mind, a purpose for living. I can honestly say that, as exciting as winning a national crown was, that amazing event pales in comparison to the night the King welcomed me into His family as His much-loved daughter.

- *Weight loss* could only change my body; it could *not* change my life.
- *Money* could only buy me things; it could *not* buy me peace of mind.
- *Success* could win me people's praises, but it could *not* heal my heart.

If Jesus is your Savior, then you have been appointed as a daughter of the King of kings. You have an amazing crown... the crown of everlasting life. You wear the most important banner of all... the banner of His name. And you may be the only Jesus some people will ever see. Yes, you have a royal responsibility to honor your King by living for Him. You have power inside of you—the King's very Spirit—to do great things for the eternal kingdom, but...

What good is being a princess if we never assume

our position of royalty in this life?

I believe if the Lord were going to personalize John 15:16 in a love letter to you, His love note might read like this...

His Princess Love Letter

My princess,

I chose you before the foundation of the earth to be My princess. You are royalty even though at times you don't feel like a princess. I will wait for you until you are ready to start living out the amazing plans that I have for you. I know that you don't know where to begin or how to live as the princess I've called you to be, so let Me teach you day by day.

Start by recognizing who I am: King of kings, Lord of lords, and the Lover of your soul. When the two of us begin to meet alone together every day, I will show you how to live as My chosen princess. But remember, My child, just as I have chosen you, I have given you a choice about whether or not to represent Me to the world. If you are willing, I am here to give you all you need to fulfill that royal calling.

Love,
Your King who has chosen you

You did not choose me,
but I chose you and appointed you to go and bear fruit—
fruit that will last.
Then the Father will give you whatever you ask in my name.

JOHN 15:16, NIV

TRUE CROWNING MOMENTS

True crowning moments in life are not those that highlight what we have accomplished for ourselves. If you think about it, once we're gone, no one will remember us for what we wore, how much we weighed, what house we lived in, or what title we held while we were here. True crowning moments in life are those that point people to our King, not ourselves.

Life has taught me this: It is…

- ⤞ our character, *not* our appearance
- ⤞ our choices, *not* our possessions
- ⤞ our courage, *not* our comfort
- ⤞ our compassion, *not* our successes

…that really matter in this life. These attributes prove we are His princess. These are the jewels that people we know and our loved ones will truly treasure when we're gone.

HIS PRINCESS IN ACTION

I had the privilege of knowing a real king's princess. Her name was Rachael, and when she was thirteen, doctors told her that cancer would take her life within eight weeks. When I called to pray with her, she said, "Would you pray that, before I die, I can share Jesus with my entire high school?" So that's what I prayed and when we got off the phone, I cried. Rachael's dying wish, her heart's desire, was not for herself, but for others. She cared more about the eternal lives of others than her own earthly life coming to an end. Rachael had an eternal perspective on life, and she was committed to representing her King and sharing His truth—despite her circumstances.

The doctors gave Rachael eight weeks, but God gave Rachael three years to live out her purpose and represent Him on her high school campus. On her sixteenth birthday, she announced, "I am ready to go home to be with the Lord. I have finished what He sent me here to do." Rachael's cancer had given her a unique and hard-to-ignore voice on her school campus. Her teachers and fellow students could not understand why this dying girl cared more about their eternal lives than her own physical life. There is never a greater time to shine for our King than when circumstances seem hopeless from a human perspective.

As the end of her life on this earth drew near, Rachael made an important request of her high school principal. She asked if the entire student body could attend her funeral, and God granted her favor with him. Her principal made buses available during school hours for anyone who wanted to attend Rachael's memorial service. I had the honor of being there, and the church was completely packed. I rejoiced as busloads of teens with a wide range of backgrounds got off those buses and entered that church. I realized that God had answered Rachael's prayer: She did get to share Jesus with her entire high school, and this letter that her pastor read was key.

> *Dear friends,*
>
> *Please do not be sad for me today, for I am in a place where there is no more sickness, no more death, and no more tears. I am in heaven, and my prayer for you is that I will see you someday in heaven. My Savior Jesus Christ has made a way for you to get here... Love, Rachael*

When the pastor finished reading Rachael's letter, he invited people to come forward and ask Jesus into their hearts. Hundreds of high school students walked down the aisles to the front of the church, kneeled by Rachael's casket, and received the crown of life. The truth is that death is not the end for the Lord's princesses, and Rachael lived out that truth as her high school watched. Truly, our God is able to do exceedingly, abundantly more than all we would ever dare to ask, hope, or dream—and that is what He did in Rachael's life. One of God's precious princesses had cancer, and she led hundreds of people to her King. I wonder how many of those students went home and told their parents about Jesus. I wonder how many will grow up and become spiritual leaders in their homes or perhaps even pastors, teachers, or evangelists.

Take a moment to ask yourself this...

- ✧ What will I be remembered for when I am gone?
- ✧ What have I contributed to the lives of those I love?
- ✧ For what do I want to be remembered?

The way we live today determines the legacy

we will leave behind us.

If you are a Christian but have never specifically asked God to use you to further His kingdom, I want to encourage you to stop and pray this prayer...

His Princess Prayer

Lord,

    Your Word tells me not to hide the eternal light You have placed in me. I'm sorry for the times I've done just that. But starting this moment I want others to know the hope You have given me. I want to have boldness to burn brightly for You in this dark world. Please help me not to hide any longer behind my fear of what others will think. Let my life reflect to the world that I am Yours. Teach me through Your Word how to live as Your daughter. I am ready to represent You.

    In Jesus' name I pray, amen.

OUR KING TAKES US FROM ORDINARY TO EXTRAORDINARY

Queen Esther was no different from you and me. She did not come from a royal bloodline, yet she is one of the greatest women in Bible history.

It was not a worldly crown that gave Esther the favor she enjoyed with King Xerxes or the power to save her people. It was her character, her courage, and her love for God that enabled her to do something great for His kingdom. She had such compassion for her people and such a passion for her calling that she willingly risked her life by standing before the king and speaking up for what was right and just. Esther's heart won her the king's respect and his willingness to listen to her, and her courage and love for others changed history.

If, like Esther, we choose to live for an audience of One—for the One who really loves us—then such crowning moments can come daily. Esther fulfilled her royal calling, and we can too. We serve the same King she did, the same King who gave Queen Esther all she needed to live out her purpose. But we cannot live as the Lord's princess in our own strength. We have to pray for our King to crown us—as He crowned Esther—with...

- ↜ COMPASSION for others.
- ↜ COURAGE to stand up for righteousness.
- ↜ CONVICTION to live for Christ.
- ↜ CHARACTER that reflects Jesus is in our hearts.
- ↜ COMMITMENT to His call on our life.

The LORD *answered, "I can do anything!*
Watch and you'll see my words come true."
NUMBERS 11:23, CEV

We will receive whatever we ask for that is according to God's will, and it is His will that these virtues become part of who we are. Our King knows how to give His Princesses the ultimate makeover; He has the *real* irresistible beauty tips. If you ask, He will give you...

A Beautiful Heart... That Is Full of His Love and Free to Love Others
There is nothing more beautiful than a woman who loves the Lord with all her heart and is free to give love to others. One seventy-year-old missionary who loved the Lord with all her heart caused me to thirst for God's love. To me she is more beautiful than any model on a magazine cover because God's love reflected through her eyes is something even the best makeup artist could never re-create. Pure, unselfish love can only happen in the power of the Holy Spirit working through us. If we will allow our King's love to accumulate deep within our souls and accept His for-giveness, we will master the art of loving others.

That Christ may dwell in your hearts through faith;
and that you, being rooted and grounded in love,
may be able to comprehend with all the saints what is
the breadth and length and height and depth,
and to know the love of Christ which surpasses knowledge,
that you may be filled up to all the fullness of God.

EPHESIANS 3:17–19, NASB

A Beautiful Mind…That Is Focused on Your Purpose

This world clouds our minds with everything but divine purpose. Almost everything we watch and read causes total confusion. Look around you—people are lost, searching for anything that makes some sense. Sadly, they are willing to do anything that imitates peace. When we are regularly spending time in the Word and prayed up, our King clears away all the confusion this world brings. He helps us live with peace in our hearts and a purpose for living beyond today. We don't have to wander around aimlessly in quest of the meaning of life. We have all we need because we belong to the King and He lavishes all the gifts of the Spirit on His beloved daughters. The richest, most famous people in the world would trade it all for what you have—the God-given power, purpose, and peace of mind you were blessed to receive on that day you met the King and became His princess.

*But the plans of the LORD stand firm forever,
the purposes of his heart through all generations.*

PSALM 33:11, NIV

*Beautiful Lips...That Speak Words of Wisdom, Encouragement,
and Life*

How blessed we are to have the power in our tongues to
speak words of life to a dying world! What an incredible
privilege to have. Our King has lined our beautiful lips to
speak words of life to a world that needs to hear about His
hope. Isn't it amazing that we, His chosen ones, have been
given the honor of impacting people's lives forever with our
words? Because we have been given this gift to speak life,
we need to ask our Lord each day to anoint our lips and put
a guard over our mouths. It is His Word spoken through us
that makes our mouths masterpieces. The world is waiting
for His princesses to speak hope and encouragement into
their lives. Ask your King to give you the words you need in
each and every circumstance...ask and He will fill your
mouth in a way that will amaze even you!

*The Sovereign LORD has given me his words of wisdom,
so that I know what to say to all these weary ones.
Morning by morning he wakens me and
opens my understanding to his will.*

ISAIAH 50:4, NLT

Beautiful Feet…That Walk with God and Lead Others to the Crown of Life

What a beautiful sight to see—a woman who walks with the Lord all her days. A woman whose life walks others to the King. When we walk through life with God-confidence, we remain as strong as our beloved King David, who walked through pain, poor choices, persecution, and success, yet somehow still managed to go down in Bible history as the man who was after the heart of God. We will all face giants that try to kill our confidence. But as long as we walk with our King, "no weapon formed against [us] will prosper"…because we are His princesses, and we are purposed to lead others to the Cross through the path of excellence found in His Word.

*How beautiful upon the mountains are the
feet of him who brings good news,
who proclaims peace, who brings glad tidings of good things,
who proclaims salvation, who says to Zion, "Your God reigns!"*

ISAIAH 52:7, NKJV

Beautiful Hands...That Reach Out to Those Who Are in Need
We are God's hands in this world, and He extends His love through our acts of kindness and generosity. The most expensive manicure in the world does not reflect the beauty of a woman that takes the time to care for others. Our hands are only truly beautiful when they are doing the work of the Lord. The amazing thing about serving others is that when a woman touches someone with her life, she begins to feel beautiful because she became a blessing.... And not many things will ever make us feel as beautiful as knowing that our King has used us as a channel of His love and grace.

She opens her hand to the poor, yes,
she reaches out her filled hands to the needy
[whether in body, mind, or spirit].
PROVERBS 31:20, AMP

Beautiful Eyes...That See with an Eternal Perspective What Matters Most
When we have an eternal view of our lives, the devil loses his power to defeat us. We know that we can conquer anything with God on our side; we know that we can survive the most challenging and painful circumstances when we realize that any situation on this earth is temporary. We'll still feel the hurt and disappointments that this life brings,

but at the same time we have God's power and peace to enable us to handle anything this fleeting life throws our way. We know that our true citizenship is in heaven.

Think of problems like being on a bad vacation: When everything goes wrong, we can find comfort and relief knowing we'll be home soon. The same is true in our spiritual journey with our King. If we know our true citizenship is in heaven, we'll stay focused on our purpose for being here and our pain and problems will grow dim in comparison to the things to come in heaven... our real home!

We never give up. Our bodies are gradually dying, but we ourselves are being made stronger each day. These little troubles are getting us ready for an eternal glory that will make all our troubles seem like nothing. Things that are seen don't last forever, but things that are not seen are eternal. That's why we keep our minds on the things that cannot be seen.

2 CORINTHIANS 4:16–18, CEV

A BEAUTIFUL LIFE THAT WILL FOREVER BE REMEMBERED

What an encouragement to know that what we do for His kingdom while we are here will never be forgotten! Because

God-given beauty is irresistible to the world. When we sincerely ask our King to help us act like His princesses, people cannot help but become influenced by the way we live our lives. He causes us to shine in this dark world, not because we are perfect, but because we are committed to Him. Earthly beauty fades and the way we look will have no impact on eternity. In Genesis 3:19, the Word warns us of this truth: "Dust you are and to dust you shall return" (AMP). But our good deeds will be treasured throughout all generations. Our King sees what we do for Him even when the world doesn't stand up and applaud. What a blessing to be part of God's great plan today and forever!

Praise the LORD! Happy are those who fear the LORD.
Yes, happy are those who delight in doing what he commands.

Their children will be successful everywhere;
an entire generation of godly people will be blessed.

They themselves will be wealthy,
and their good deeds will never be forgotten.

PSALM 112:1–3, NLT

DON'T MISS YOUR CROWNING
MOMENT—OUR REIGN IS NOW!

We have been crowned with forgiveness, salvation, and acceptance into God's kingdom. Because His Spirit is in us, we are now adorned with His beauty. Now is the time to shine for Him—let's not miss a moment of what He has for us to do! Remember, just as God placed Queen Esther in the court of King Xerxes so that she could save her people, our heavenly King has put us in a particular place in order to save people who don't yet know Him. We are appointed to be His princesses for such a time as this. Our reign is now! Put on your God-appointed crown and take your royal position.

But you are the ones chosen by God, chosen for the high calling of priestly work, chosen to be a holy people, God's instruments to do his work and speak out for him, to tell others of the night-and-day difference he made for you— from nothing to something, from rejected to accepted. Friends, this world is not your home, so don't make yourselves cozy in it. Don't indulge your ego at the expense of your soul. Live an exemplary life among the natives so that your actions will refute their prejudices. Then they'll be won over to God's side and be there to join in the celebration when he arrives.

1 PETER 2:9–12, *THE MESSAGE*

HIS PRINCESS IN ACTION

1. We won't wear a golden crown or carry a scepter as we do what God has called us to do, and this royal call is not about our accomplishments. Our Prince has done it all: He died on the cross for our sins so that we can begin our eternal reign while we are here. Our reign is all about our confidence in our King and about investing our time and God-given talents in eternity.

2. You and I came into this world with nothing, and we will leave with nothing except the legacy of those we lead to the Lord. The only significant thing we will leave behind us is our witness for Jesus and the memory of a life lived in faith in Him. So don't let the devil distract you for another moment. Choose to make your life matter for all eternity. Don't let anything or anyone keep you from your calling! And remember that it was *not* the crown on her head that made Esther a great queen. It was her heart for her God and her people and her willingness to serve Him. So live for your King, and He will crown you in His glory for all to see you are His.

3. Loving God and loving others will always put us in a position of influence. The world is searching for a real faith in the true God. So shine for your King, starting now!

Remember this...

I want it to be here ↵

A worldly princess glorifies herself	His princess glorifies her King
A worldly princess cares about her needs and desires	His princess is more concerned about the needs of others
A worldly princess will be known for her comfortable way of life	His princess will be remembered for her character and her courage
A worldly princess invests her time and talent in the here and now	His princess invests in eternity
The self-centered reign of a worldly princess will end	The God-focused reign of His princess will last forever

Anyone can choose to be a worldly princess, but you have been handpicked by the King to be His princess. So take your royal position starting today!

PRINCESSES ARE NOT PERFECT... THE PRESSURE IS OFF

I know how hard it is for us to think of ourselves as royalty. Each of us knows our weaknesses and imperfections all too well! So let me take the pressure off you: No man or woman in the Bible or in Christian history, no believer who did something great to further God's kingdom, lived a perfect life. The key to their accomplishing something significant for God was the simple fact that they loved the Lord. They were committed to Him and to answering His call on their life despite their failures, despite difficult circumstances, and despite people who hurt them or discouraged them.

God is *not* looking for perfect princesses to do His work on earth. Instead, He is looking for our heart-commitment to Him. It's truly wonderful that we don't have to be perfect to be our King's princess or to earn His love and approval. Our King loves us no matter how many times we fall. In fact, He is always there to pick us up, heal our hearts, and help us start walking again.

Even if godly people fall down seven times,
they always get up.
PROVERBS 24:16,
NEW INTERNATIONAL READER'S VERSION

I was eighteen years old when I entered my first beauty pageant and competed for the Miss San Jose crown. My father was a Hollywood DJ who had hosted beauty pageants when I was a little girl. So I had spent a lot of time watching girls walk down the runway doing that famous pageant wave. Now I would be doing just that, and, having lost sixty pounds in preparation for the competition, I was especially excited about the evening gown segment.

I was all dressed up and ready to walk down that glamorously lit runway. I did my little wave, smiled as big as I could, and gracefully strolled toward the judges. With my elegant gown, my lovely shoes, and my newly thin body, I was feeling so graceful—until I came to the end of the runway and fell off the stage right onto the judges' table. Everyone in the audience gasped! But as I lay there flat on my face, do you know what I was thinking? I was thinking, *I still want to win!*

The truth is…we all fall down at some point in life. Sometimes another person pushes us down. At other times we set ourselves up for failure by disobeying our King. And I've discovered that we all want to win and we can win, despite our falls, if we let the Lord help us get back up again.

So don't let anyone ever tell you that God cannot redeem what you have done. You were born again to win victory in every area of your life! So ask the Lord to help you get up and let Him handle whoever and whatever is keeping you down—and you'll win!

Well, I wanted to win the Miss San Jose crown, so I got off the judges' table, stood up on that stage, and said boldly, "I just wanted to make sure you would remember me." The audience rose to their feet and applauded loudly. Believe it or not, I did end up winning the crown that night. After the pageant the judges came up to me and said that they chose me because they were so impressed by the way I recovered from my fall.

I didn't know the Lord then, but I know Him now. I took quite a fall in that pageant, but I have taken many worse falls since that very embarrassing moment. Those falls have hurt me and others. But every time I've thought, *I can't get up again,* I cried out to my King. He has always heard me, and He has always stretched out His hand to help me stand up and continue reigning for Him.

I tell you about my Miss San Jose pageant because I learned a very important life lesson that night. I learned that it is not only how we act that makes a difference in our lives; it is also how we choose to react to pain, disappointment, and rejection that will determine whether we win or lose in this life! However good the news is, if we did not react the right way, we can come to our King and repent and pray for wisdom on what to do now.

Keep in mind that there is not a soul on this earth who won't experience failure, disappointment, and discouragement, but the good news is this: Our King is able to do exceedingly more than we would ever dare to ask, hope, or dream (Ephesians 3:20).

Remember King David? When he was just a shepherd boy, his father Jesse didn't even consider him a candidate when the prophet Samuel told him that one of his sons would be king of Israel. Yet it was the young shepherd who had the faith and courage to step onto the battlefield and face Goliath, and David faced the armed giant with nothing more than some stones and a sling—and his God!

This was the same King David who, years later, wasn't strong enough to walk away from temptation. He took another man's wife and then, to cover his sin, had her soldier-husband killed. The same God who gave David the strength to kill Goliath is the same God who forgave David's sin. And redemption doesn't stop there: The same woman who committed adultery with David is the same woman who was mother to King Solomon, the wisest man who ever lived.

Take a moment to pray this prayer...

His Princess Prayer

Dear Jesus,

I confess that I am weak without You, and I confess my lack of commitment to the call You have on my life. Please forgive me. And please help me trust You more. Remind me, Lord, how powerful You are in comparison to any giant—internal or external—that I will face. Give me the strength to get back up when I fall and the courage to stand for what is right in Your sight. I affirm this day my commitment to walk with You, and I ask You to provide all that I need to finish strong this race of faith.

In Jesus' name I pray, amen.

You have just cemented, if not completely changed, the course of your *spiritual life* with a prayer.

DON'T MISS YOUR CROWNING MOMENT

The first time I was invited to share my story, I felt completely unqualified to speak, especially in front of four hundred women's ministry leaders. *Each of them must be totally without sin, or they wouldn't be in such a leadership position,* I thought. (Back then I was not familiar with the scriptural truth that all have sinned and fallen short of God's glory [Romans 3:32]!)

The invitation to speak came from a woman who had totally humiliated me at the dinner table in front of my husband's Bible professors. There I was, thoroughly enjoying the company and conversation, when this woman said loudly, "I heard you were fat, Jewish, and on drugs. How did you *ever* become a Christian?" Of course all eyes were suddenly on me. These people wanted to hear the juicy details of my life, and I felt pressured to share my testimony. When I finished, I wanted to run out of that room as fast as my feet could carry me—and never see those people again.

I didn't realize that that embarrassing night was the crowning moment when God birthed my speaking ministry. The very woman who humiliated me at dinner later invited me to share my story in front of that group of Christian leaders. God has a strange way of calling each of us, but if we could easily and completely understand all His ways, then we would not need faith or trust. Now I absolutely love to share my story of God's goodness and redemption, but I would have missed this opportunity if I had let my own insecurities and my anger with that woman get the better of me—and get in the way of God's will for my life.

So don't doubt God! He has chosen you and me to be His princesses, and we need to take Him at His word. We are all called to make a difference while we are here and to further His Kingdom. How this truth unfolds in our lives is up to our King. We need to walk with confidence in the King, not in our self. If we truly want our lives to matter for eternity, then we better start acting and living like His princesses or we will miss our crowning moment. Don't wait until you figure out His specific calling for you. Instead, do right now what you know He requires of us all: to live according to His Word and trust Him to make your next steps clear in His perfect way and time. After all, He is the King.

Mary, the Mother of Jesus…
Could have missed her crowning moment if she had feared what others—including her fiancé, Joseph—would think of her. But this teenage virgin took the step of faith and believed that the Holy Spirit had placed our Savior in her womb. She was able to do so because she loved and trusted her Lord more than she feared for her future. What an example of humble service and great faith she is to us two thousand years later!

*A*nd Mary said:
"My soul glorifies the Lord
and my spirit rejoices in God my Savior,
for he has been mindful
of the humble state of his servant.
From now on all generations will call me blessed,
for the Mighty One has done great things for me—
holy is his name."

LUKE 1:46–49, NIV

King David...
Could have missed his crowning moment had he seized an opportunity to take revenge against Saul. A little background... Before David was crowned king, the reigning King Saul was horribly jealous of him because God's favor was so clearly upon this brave and handsome warrior. So Saul decided to try to kill David. This future king was torn from the many comforts he was accustomed to and forced to hide out in caves to protect his very life. I'm sure David must have wondered, *Is this really God's will for me?*

But rather than let his doubts keep him from obeying God's call on his life, David did two things that prepared him to be a great king. First, he transferred his pain into prayer and cried out to God in writing. Today those pain-filled prayers, found in the book of Psalms, show us how to be open and honest with our heavenly King. Second, David resisted the temptation to kill his enemy even when he came upon the sleeping Saul. From a human perspective, David had good reason to kill Saul. He had made David's life miserable and now was seeking to kill him; Saul was after David without a just reason. Even Saul's son Jonathan took David's side during the hunt. But David, the anointed king, did something much greater than take revenge: He deferred to God's will and obeyed the command not to strike down the man God had placed on the throne. Obediently submitting to God was more important to David than exacting revenge.

Many of us will never experience the magnitude of God's great call on our lives until we give revenge back to the Lord. Is there a King Saul in your life—someone you need to leave to God's care even though you have real reasons to act in revenge? Follow King David's example and let God deal with those who have caused you pain and suffering. When we do so, we find the freedom that comes with doing what is right in God's sight. He will deal with those who have hurt His daughters!

Take comfort in these words from our almighty and just Father in heaven:

*Never avenge yourselves. Leave that to God. For it is written,
"I will take vengeance; I will repay those who deserve it," says the Lord.*

ROMANS 12:19, NLT

The Apostle Peter...

Could have missed his crowning moment because of guilt. Peter loved Jesus passionately, but when the time came for him to stand up for his Savior, Peter denied Him not once, not twice, but three times. If Peter had not accepted God's forgiveness, then he might have spent his entire life paralyzed by guilt rather than helping other Jews realize that Jesus was their long-awaited Messiah.

When we let guilt keep us paralyzed from living out our purpose, we are saying by our actions that the cross was not enough to set us free from guilt from our past mistakes. Praise be to our God, we are a new creation. As far as the east is from the west is how far He has removed our sins from us—and remembers them no more. Do not let the devil whisper lies that you are still guilty—let your Lord whisper His truth that you are totally forgiven and a brand-new creation in Christ.

Finally, I confessed all my sins to you and stopped trying to hide them.
I said to myself, "I will confess my rebellion to the LORD."
And you forgave me! All my guilt is gone.

PSALM 32:5, NLT

The Apostle Paul...

Could have missed his crowning moment because of prideful arrogance. Physical blindness humbled him, and persecution and pain enabled him to share the gospel and build up Christ's church. After only some of his many beatings, imprisonments, and other hardships, Paul could have said, "I don't deserve all this," but then he would have missed all that God had created him for and called him to. Paul had the awesome privilege of teaching and equipping the Gentiles in his day—and, through his many New Testament writings, us, centuries later—for a life of holiness.

True crowning moments—like the ones Mary, David, Peter, Paul, and you and I experienced—are not just about the here and now. Crowning moments, when God opens our eyes to His love for us and His specific plan for us—are about future generations and eternity. Our world desperately needs to see God in us. This is not the time for us to worry about our comfort. It is the time for us to turn to God for the courage and conviction we need to shine His light for those who are still living in darkness. Do not forget His promise: If we love and obey Him, our lives will impact a thousand generations (Deuteronomy 7:9). And don't miss what God has for you: When we serve Him, we are blessed as He uses us to bless others. So take this moment right now to let go of anything that is holding you back from the glorious future your King has for you. Absolutely nothing this world has to offer can compare to God's blessings and favor to do great things while you are here.

What an honor to be God's princesses—and we didn't have to compete for the crown. Our King has chosen us, and we didn't need to do anything to win His attention, His favor, or His love. You have already won His heart, and He has gifted you personally to do something great for His kingdom!

Take a moment to pray this prayer...

3/12/2009

His Princess Prayer

Dear Jesus,

Please help me remember that I am a part of Your forever kingdom and Your eternal plan. Open my eyes to Your majesty and love so that I will see myself as royalty. Do not let me waste another day not living for You and not loving You with all my heart. I give You all that I am. Align my dreams and goals with Your perfect plan for me. Help me let go of anything that is keeping me from obeying You and knowing Your blessings. I love You, Lord, and I want to show You my love with my life. I choose on this day to take my royal position as Your light to the world.

In Jesus' name I pray, amen.

As this chapter ends, remember that…

- ↬ our character,
- ↬ our convictions,
- ↬ our courage,
- ↬ our caring,

- ❧ our compassion,
- ❧ our choices, and
- ❧ our commitment to our King

determine our legacy. Remember, too, that:

- ❧ Our King has empowered us so that, like Rachael, we can do the work He placed us here to do.
- ❧ No one can take away our God-given crown of purpose and power.
- ❧ Anything you do for your King will have eternal rewards that will be beyond anything we could ever imagine and will be revealed for all to see when our King welcomes us to our home in heaven.

So I encourage you to go to your King every day, meet Him in His Word, and speak to Him with prayer and praise so that, wearing your God-given crown, you are able to shine brightly for Him and finish what you were sent here to do!

And never forget the truth of God's Word....

*Out of all the peoples on the face of the earth,
the LORD has chosen you to be his treasured possession.*
DEUTERONOMY 14:2, NIV

Warrior for the King

LIVING IN THE FREEDOM
HE HAS WON

For the LORD your God is going with you!
He will fight for you against your enemies, and he will give you victory!

DEUTERONOMY 20:4, NLT

ur Prince loves us so passionately that He gave His life so that we may live in total freedom from guilt, anger, and pain rooted in our past; from the problems in our present; and from fear of our future. He paid too great a price on that cross for us to live defeated, powerless lives!

In order to live in the freedom which Jesus won for us on the cross, we will need a battle plan—and our King has given us just that. Praise God for His Word and its winning plan for living a victorious life—victorious over the world, the flesh, and the devil; victorious over sin; victorious over darkness and hopelessness. He desires with great compassion for us to know and live in that dearly bought freedom.

If God wrote Deuteronomy 31:6 in a personal letter just to His Princesses, it would read something like this...

His Princess Love Letter

Dear Princess,

I long for you to know freedom from guilt and anger, from fear and worry, from hopelessness and purposelessness. I loved you with My life so that you can be free of such things. Nothing in this world—nothing except you yourself, My love—can keep you from walking in My freedom. So come to Me and read My Word. Cry out to Me, My love, and I will give you the keys to living in freedom. You will become My princess warrior when you pray and obey My voice.... I will never hurt you or leave you alone, so come to Me, My daughter, and I, your Daddy in heaven, will soothe your soul, restore your peace of mind, and set your precious feet on solid ground.

Love, your King and your Freedom, Jesus

"Be strong and courageous. Do not be afraid or terrified...
for the LORD your God goes with you;
he will never leave you nor forsake you."

DEUTERONOMY 31:6, NIV

Many of us know the Lord personally but feel anything but free or victorious. Have you ever wondered, *If God loves me, then why does He allow me to experience pain?*

There are different perspectives on why God allows pain. But here is some truth about some of the pain we experience in this life: We are in a spiritual battle against an unseen enemy out to destroy our very souls (Ephesians 6:12). Our King warns us in His Word that the enemy of our soul is looking for any opportunity to steal from us, destroy us, and ultimately kill us. Satan is like a roaring lion waiting for the perfect time to attack, but take courage in this truth:

NO WEAPON FORMED AGAINST
US WILL PROSPER...
unless we step out from behind God's shield
of protection around us
by fighting in our own strength and our own way!

Sometimes the pain we feel in life is a result of this raging spiritual battle, but God can and will bring good out of pain, whatever its cause. Our King uses pain to develop within us the qualities He knows we will need to complete our purpose for eternity. He also uses our pain to draw us closer to Him, to grow compassion for others, and to strengthen our character. Pain can be the boot camp that prepares us for our purpose. Pain can be used to show others how to fight the good fight. It is also used to experience victory in His power. Just think about a trail in your life that ended in a deeper walk with Him and has made you a better person as a result. As painful as it was at the time, can you look back now and see the mighty work He was able to do in you and through you for His glory? What about an impossible problem for which you thought there was no solution, and then God showed up and your confidence in your King was greatly increased?

I used to feel angry with God for allowing me to grow up in such a dysfunctional home. Why hadn't He put me in a family that lived together peacefully? Why did He let me cry myself to sleep at night while my parents screamed at each other in the other room? Why did other little girls have parents who loved each other and got along?

I don't think it was God's will that my parents fought or that their marriage ended in divorce. But today I realize that my past pain and my parents' marital problems do not have to determine my future. God had a plan for me then, and He has used my painful past to make me passionate for peace in my own family now. He has used my parents' divorce to compel me to stay married when times have gotten tough in my own marriage. He has used my poor choices to take drugs by giving me courage to speak to young people about how to live for our King. My battle with bulimia drove me to write a bestselling book that helps girls and women break free from that bondage. Our God can take any part of our lives, good or bad, and use it to further His kingdom. We can be a trophy of His grace, forgiveness, and neverending mercy for the world to see.

God causes everything to work together for the good of those who love God and are called according to his purpose for them... to become like his Son.
ROMANS 8:28–29, NLT

If everything in my life had gone the way I wanted it to, I might not have such passion for my God-given call as a Christian speaker, and I might not have such heartfelt compassion for those who have walked through similar trials in this life. I probably would not have used my Mrs. USA crown to tell the world about my King. God used my past to prepare me for ministry. However, if I could go back and live my life God's way, of course I would—but that is not an option. So I have a choice: I can remain paralyzed by pain, guilt, anger, and regret, or I can let God use my past mistakes as tutors to make me wiser and to help me teach others. I'm choosing the second option, and I have learned to be grateful for every trial and every tear because God has used them to develop me into the person He wants me to be. Although my life is not perfect, it is complete in Christ, and I can honestly say that I am totally free of guilt, anger, and regret from the past because my past is where it belongs... nailed to the Cross!

We are so blessed to serve a King who turns our sorrow into joy and our pain into purpose.

For he has rescued us from the dominion of darkness and brought us into the kingdom of the Son he loves, in whom we have redemption, the forgiveness of sins.
COLOSSIANS 1:13–14, NIV

God has rescued us from the darkness of sin and guilt, of pointless pain and burning anger. He will always make a way when there doesn't seem to be one. We do not have to live in discouragement, depression, defeat, or hopelessness.

We can live victorious lives in Christ—in His redemptive love and power. We can be His bold princess warriors—and He will help us win the spiritual battles that try and overtake our minds and emotions. One of the deceiver's favorite tricks is to make us feel that all is hopeless, but the truth is that the Lord will give us victory!

Remember the Israelites? God rescued them and brought them out of slavery in Egypt—and immediately to the edge of the Red Sea. There the chosen, rescued people stood, stuck between what looked like a sea of hopelessness and their enemies charging toward them. I am sure they felt abandoned and defeated, and we know they questioned why God had set them free if they were going to die defeated by their Egyptian enemies. However, it was that apparently hopeless situation that God used to destroy their Egyptian enemies once and for all! And that sea of hopelessness gave God another opportunity to prove His power: He parted the waters and His people walked on dry land to their freedom. Then He closed the waters, and Israel watched her enemies die before their very eyes. Sometimes life's greatest trials give us greater faith. The Israelites did *not* have to do anything to see victory except walk to their freedom through the open door their God provided.

HIS BATTLE PLAN FOR FREEDOM

America is a free country because, through the years, our soldiers have gone to war and fought for our freedom. Men and women alike have sacrificed their lives so that we may live free. And when they went off to battle, they went with passion, purpose, and a plan.

The Word of the Lord (the Bible) is filled with true stories about real battles against God's people, and in every battle our King gives a plan for victory. However, He also gives His people a choice to win His way or to be defeated by fighting their way. I pray as we study His plan for our freedom that you will choose life... His way!

At the end of our days on this earth, wouldn't it be great to be able to say, as Paul did,

*I have fought a good fight, I have finished the race,
and I have remained faithful. And now the prize awaits me—
the crown of righteousness that the Lord, the righteous Judge, will give
me on that great day of his return. And the prize is not just for me
but for all who eagerly look forward to his glorious return.*

2 TIMOTHY 4:7–8, NLT

I cannot imagine anything better than knowing that we have accomplished what God sent us here to do! The goal of this chapter is to help us learn how to fight the greatest battle of all—the battle in our mind and emotions that keeps us from living out the victorious life that is already ours. If we don't know our King's battle plan or the weapons and protection He has for us, we will be defeated again and again. It is time to claim the victory that is rightfully ours!

Our first step toward freedom is choosing to let our Lord be our Leader in life. Let's take this step through prayer…

His Princess Prayer

Dear Jesus,

I choose on this day to surrender my past, my pain, and my problems to You. I ask You to help me see Your plan for my freedom. Give me wisdom and courage to walk through all of life's battles with You. I pray in faith, believing that You have already won my freedom for me and trusting You to fight for me and give me victory in every area of my life. I love You, and I thank You for all You have already done for me and all that You will do for me.

In Your name I pray, amen.

FREEDOM—FIND THE ROOT
OF THE PAIN OR PROBLEM

If we don't find out what's causing us pain or problems, then it will end up controlling us. Pretending that our pain isn't real won't make it go away. In fact, if we continue to ignore our hurts, no matter how long ago or how recently they happened, they will defeat us. I know from experience. I used to pretend so well that I could have earned an Oscar for Best Actress and a doctoral degree in denial. Can you relate? That kind of acting and denying is easier than looking openly and honestly at what has happened to us and at its continuing impact on us. Sometimes it is so hard to look honestly at those hurts, but the only way to complete healing is the path of truth! Remember God's promise, "Those who sow with tears will reap with joy." People ask me again and again after I speak about my life: "How did you get past the pain?" My answer is, "Every time it hurt I cried out to my Daddy in heaven, and every tear began cleansing my soul."

I also know how hard it is to find the time to heal. The list of demands on us as wives and mothers, as homemakers and cooks, as tutors and chauffeurs, as personal shoppers and school volunteers can seem endless. These demands wear us out, and our exhaustion affects us emotionally. We find ourselves discouraged and depressed. And putting more pressure on us, some well-meaning Christians have said that we need to ignore our feelings and live by faith. My question to them is this: If we are supposed to ignore our feelings, then why did God give them to us in the first place? He created us in His image. He has feelings, and we do too. Did you know that the Bible refers to God's emotions more than two thousand times?

Ephesians 4:26 says, "Be angry, and yet do not sin" (NASB). It is not a sin to feel angry, hurt, overwhelmed, or out of control. It becomes a sin if we don't deal with the feelings and let them affect our actions. The way to deal with our feelings—the only way to get out from under their control of us—is to find out what is causing them. Unfortunately many of us have hidden our hurts so deeply in our hearts that we don't feel anything at all anymore, so we struggle to identify what is causing our actions or reactions in many situations. If that's the case, it's time to fall on our faces and cry out to the all-knowing, living God that truly loves us and wants to heal us—the One who knows everything that's hidden in our hearts.

Not knowing why we're feeling what we're feeling is only one part of the problem. Another part of the problem is not knowing how to deal with what we are feeling. That's another reason we don't deal with our feelings. But pretending that pain is not real is like pretending that your car doesn't need gas. Even if we ignore all the warning signs, we will still run out of gas. Likewise, we can't win the battle in our mind or the spiritual war with the devil if we ignore the warning signs and continue running on empty inside. Warning lights are God's way of telling us that we need Him—His grace, His truth, His healing, His comfort. I know from personal experience how hard it is to deal with the truth about our lives and ourselves, but truth plus tears leads to freedom from the past. I once heard that tears are wet prayers. We can know true freedom if we will stop pretending that our pain doesn't exist and if we start being open and honest with ourselves and our Lord.

A man is a slave to whatever has mastered him.
2 PETER 2:19, NIV

Finding out what has mastered us, what is controlling us, is our first step toward our freedom. So stop and take a personal inventory of your feelings.

Right now I feel: 8/13/09

- Afraid of the future
- Angry
- Impatient
- Out of control
- Exhausted
- Addicted to the approval of others 8/13/09
- Unappreciated
- Depressed
- Hopeless
- Lonely *miss Leo + maya 8/13/09*
- Numb inside
- Anxious
- Unhealthy
- Overwhelmed 8/13/09
- Unloved

Let's be open and honest right now in a prayer to our King.

His Princess Prayer

Dear Jesus,

I feel (fill in what you feel: _distracted lonely_), and I don't want to live in this emotional place any longer. As frightening as this is for me right now, I pray, Father God, that You would reveal the root of my unhealthy actions and reactions. I need You to show me what is going on inside of me so that I can give my heart and all of its hurts to You. I want to change, and I ask You to intervene now and show me what I need to do to be healed and whole. I am ready to let You remove the root of my pain. Thank You for being my safe place, and thank You that I can come to You with anything. I love You and I praise You for Your faithfulness to me. Now, by the work of Your Holy Spirit, please help me.

In Your name I pray, amen.

When God helps you recognize the root of your feelings, write down what you discover. Writing it down makes it become real, and it gives you a touchstone for taking the next step toward freedom.

"Then you will know the truth, and the truth will set you free."

Now that we have used the first key to our freedom and written it down, we will begin to remove the root causing our pain by taking our next step toward freedom.

FREEDOM — RUN TO GOD

The LORD hears his people when they call to him for help.
He rescues them from all their troubles.

Once you discover the root of your feelings, you may hurt even more than when you were hiding those feelings. Know that in order to truly be healed, you have to feel that pain. In your pain, cry out to your King until He wipes away every tear. I promise He will.

King David cried out to God every time he was hurting, and he is known as "a man after God's own heart." We find another example of honesty before God in King Hezekiah. He was on his deathbed when he prayed and wept bitterly before the Lord. God heard his prayers, saw his tears, and healed him. If you truly want to be a woman after God's own heart and want to know the complete healing God offers you, then run to Him every time you hurt. He is your Daddy in heaven, and He longs to comfort and heal you.

Then Jesus said, "Come to me, all of you who are weary and carry heavy burdens, and I will give you rest."
MATTHEW 11:28, NLT

No one can heal your heart or soothe your soul like your King can. No one loves you more, and no one else has the power or passion for you that your God has. He is the Lover of your soul, and He longs for you to run to Him so that He can heal your every hurt.

HIS PRINCESS LOVE LETTER

My Princess...

I am your Shield of Protection. Many times you wonder where I am in the midst of the battle that rages around you. You feel abandoned on the battlefield. Don't be afraid and don't lose faith. I am here, and I am always victorious. I will protect you, but you must trust Me. Sometimes I will lead you to shelter for safety and restoration. Other times I will ask you to join Me on the front lines in the heat of the battle. I can kill any giant that threatens your life, but, as David the shepherd boy did, you need to march forward, pick up the stones, and face your enemy. I love to prove My strength when the odds against Me are the greatest and hope is the smallest. I am truly your Shelter and your Deliverer, and I will protect you no matter where you are.

Love, your King and your Protector

You are my hiding place;
you will protect me from trouble
and surround me with songs of deliverance.

PSALM 32:7, NIV

Our God is our place of rest, our safe place. When we are in His presence, He will restore our mind, our body, and our soul.

After you find the root and run to the King with your hurts, the next step toward freedom is praising Him despite your pain. In fairy tales that I've heard, the princesses always seem to maintain hope in the middle of the most miserable circumstances. They somehow know that their prince will rescue them—and he always does. As God's princess, you have His promise and you can completely trust that your Prince will rescue you. That confident hope is a key to joy and to the ability to praise Him even in the tough times.

Acts 16 gives us a beautiful illustration of what can happen when we praise our Prince in the midst of our trials and tribulations. Paul and Silas, two faithful men of God, were unjustly thrown into prison for boldly sharing God's message of hope. They could have been angry at God for not protecting them, they could have been worried about their future or their very lives, or they could choose to trust the King in their trial and praise Him despite their circumstances. Paul and Silas chose to praise God from a cold, ugly prison cell with songs of praise.

According to Scripture, other prisoners heard and listened as these faithful followers sang songs of love to their

Lord. Suddenly there was a great earthquake, and the prison was shaken to its foundation. The doors flew open, and the chains fell off of every prisoner. (Something supernatural happens when, in the midst of battle, we choose to offer a sacrifice of praise to our King!) Not only were Paul and Silas set free from their chains, but every prisoner who was listening and watching their reaction to a bad situation was set free.

This prison scene shows us one reason why it is so important for us to be open and honest when we are struggling: Our reactions affect people around us either for good or not so good. It's also important for us to be open and honest with our children when we are struggling. Of course we don't have to give them every detail, but we can have them pray and praise God with us so that they will see for themselves God's mighty hand move in a tough situation. If we take our children to the King in our times of trouble, when they grow up and experience their own pain and problems, they will know exactly what to do and whom to turn to. (If we don't show them, who will?) Also, our openness will encourage our children to develop a completely honest and personal relationship with the Lord. No one benefits from the "my life is perfect" or the "I can handle it myself" Christian act. Everyone benefits when we acknowledge that life is not perfect but God is. Everyone benefits from seeing us run to God and praise Him despite our pain and problems—and then seeing that He gives us perfect peace.

King David cried out to God and praised Him in all seasons of his life. Read these words written by the man after God's heart....

He has given me a new song to sing,
a hymn of praise to our God.
Many will see what he has done and be astounded.
They will put their trust in the LORD.

PSALM 40:3, NLT

Praise is not denying the problem.

Praise is looking to God as the power and solution.

When you go into battle in your own land
against an enemy who is oppressing you,
sound a blast on the trumpets. Then you will be remembered by
the LORD your God and rescued from your enemies.

NUMBERS 10:9, NIV

Sometimes our biggest battles happen in the land of our own homes. Therefore we need to get up in the morning and enter into the King's presence with praise. If you are prayed up and praising God in song at the start of each day, you will set a tone of joy and hope and victory in your home. Remember that our homes are on the top of the enemy's hit list, so cover your family through prayer and put on praise music first thing in the morning!

FREEDOM—Edit Your Life

Fix your thoughts on what is true and honorable and right.
Think about things that are pure and lovely and admirable.
Think about things that are excellent and worthy of praise.

PHILIPPIANS 4:8, NLT

After you have identified the root of your pain or problem and are choosing to run to God and praise Him through any and all healing and deliverance, it is time for you to taste real victory by editing the enemy's weapons out of your life.

If a police officer came to your door and warned you that your neighbors had just been robbed and killed, you would be on the lookout for anything that could let that enemy in your home or near your loved ones. Our King warns us in His Word that there is an enemy after us (John 10:10) and he is out to kill, steal, and destroy us, and that if we are not careful we will help him accomplish his mission by what we read, watch, and listen to. We will let him destroy our values, our minds, and our children through the modern entertainment we allow in our homes.

If our soldiers went into battle unarmed and drunk, they would be the laughingstock of the world. If we really want freedom and victory, then we cannot compromise by our words and actions whom we represent and what we say we believe. We are called to live holy lives and be examples of excellence in this lost and lonely world, looking for someone to follow. Our lives can become louder than the world's influence. We do not have to give in to temptation; we are warriors of the King and have been given the power to live like the royalty we are called to be. It is not that our King does not want us to have any fun or entertainment; He does not want His daughters' minds to be destroyed!

Here are some royal training tips:

EDIT WHAT YOU READ

How do you feel about yourself after you have read a fashion magazine? Are you thinking, *I am fearfully and wonderfully made by God,* or *I feel so secure about my body—and myself—now that I have looked at air-brushed models?* No one feels good about who they are or how they look in comparison to the four-color glossy man-made fashion idols. (The models don't even look as good as those photos in real life!) Besides, why should we let our image be defined by the worldly men or women who produce magazines that stand for everything except holiness and godliness? Our worth is not determined by what we weigh, and while on her deathbed, no woman is going to be thinking, *I just wish I could have had thinner thighs and bigger breasts.*

Rather than filling our minds with images and idols of the world, we need to read things that give us and our daughters passion for our purpose and strength to respond in obedience to God's call on our life. We women beat ourselves up enough for what we are not. We definitely don't need to help the enemy finish off any shred of confidence that may be hanging on inside of us. So don't open the wrong kind of reading material and thereby open the door for the devil to prey on your thoughts or the thoughts of those you love. And remember that you are here for such a time as this: You are the King's princess, called to shine for His glory.

How foolish are those who manufacture idols to be their gods.
These highly valued objects are really worthless.
They themselves are witnesses that this is so,
for their idols neither see nor know.
No wonder those who worship them are put to shame.

ISAIAH 44:9, NLT

Get rid of any books or magazines that threaten your identity in Christ and cause you to feel shame about how God made you. Don't allow these worthless idols to determine your worth. You and I are daughters of the King, and we are to model His true beauty for the world. No one will ever remember the cover girls when their time of fame comes to an end. Unless we invest in the lives of others, our beauty is worthless and it will not last.

EDIT WHAT YOU WATCH

We live in a town so small that I think we have only one Yellow Page. I lived in Southern California and Scottsdale, Arizona, prior to moving to this tiny town in Oregon. Needless to say, there is not a lot to do. So it would be very tempting to get cable TV, but I have a husband, a teenage son, and a five-year-old daughter...

But it occurred to me one day that, if I agreed to pay

thirty dollars a month to receive several hundred channels, I would be opening the door of our home to the enemy; I would essentially be inviting him in so that he could attack and undermine the godly values and priorities I'm trying to instill in my children. And he could steal my relationship with my husband, who might easily pay more attention to the television than to our children or me.

As if all that wouldn't be dangerous and damaging enough, my son and husband would be exposed to images of sex, women, and violence over one hundred times an hour as they flipped through the channels. My little daughter would learn to disrespect me as she watched cartoons and sitcoms that portray children as disrespectful and running the household, and parents as idiots.

Now, I'm not saying that all television is bad. My Jewish family came to know the Lord through Christian television. But why would we pay to allow images in our home that stand for everything we don't? Besides, we have only a very short time to talk with and teach our children, and in the busyness of life we have very little time to be with our husbands. How are we spending this valuable time? Are hours of television going to draw us closer to God, to our loved ones, and to fulfilling our purpose on this planet? Will those hours in front of the television help us reach the next generation and the world around us for Christ?

Today television, computers, and game boxes take up so much time and energy that many young people don't know how to look in a person's eyes and have a conversation. It is our responsibility to prepare the young people in our homes to be godly husbands or wives and the King's ambassadors in the world. If we let the television teach them how to live, we are setting them up for failure and heartache.

I admit that there are some great television shows I'd like to watch, but I would not trade the time I spend with my family talking and laughing and praying together for the most entertaining program in the world. Sometimes we have to trade what we want at the moment for what we want most. And I have found that exchanging television for time with my family is definitely worth the trade!

Like our forefathers in the faith, we can choose to say...

As for me and my household, we will serve the LORD.

JOSHUA 24:15, NIV

Sometimes we have to trade what we want at the moment for what we want most.

His Princess Prayer

Dear Lord,

*Please show me what I am reading and
watching that is keeping me from You. Help me see
what I am allowing in my home for what it is—
and then give me the courage and conviction to say
no to what I shouldn't be allowing. Grant me the
self-discipline to give up whatever You ask me to
surrender and, starting today, to read and watch
that which will build my faith and character.
Forgive me for anything sinful that I have allowed
to enter my mind, and I pray in faith that You will
transform me and cleanse me from the inside out.*

In Jesus' name I pray, amen.

*D*on't copy the behavior and customs of this world,
but let God transform you into a new person by changing the way you think.
Then you will know what God wants you to do, and you will know how
good and pleasing and perfect his will really is.

R O M A N S   1 2 : 2 ,   N L T

Watch your thoughts—they become your words.

Watch your words—they become your actions.

Watch your actions—they become your habits.

Watch your habits—they become your character.

Watch your character—it becomes your legacy.

I will lead a life of integrity in my own home.
I will refuse to look at anything vile and vulgar.
PSALM 101:2-3, NLT

EDIT YOUR SCHEDULE

The enemy doesn't have to completely defeat us in order to win the battle for our energy and time. All he has to do is distract us, and his victory comes easily. And we know distraction, don't we? Nothing burns us women out more than excessive busyness. No time to rest, relax, reflect, or restore ourselves. Somehow we feel—consciously or otherwise—

that if our schedules aren't packed with places to go, people to see, and endless things to do, we must not be important. Or maybe we are so concerned about what others will think that we are not willing to set healthy boundaries. When my schedule gets overloaded, my family suffers, my health suffers, and my relationship with God suffers. The devil wants us weak on all these fronts because then he can take us down.

Keep in mind that "if the devil can't make us bad, his next trick is to make us busy." If we are too busy to spend time with God or too busy to spend time with the loved ones who need us, then we are busier than our King wants us to be. We need to set our schedule so that it accurately reflects our priorities. To help you determine those priorities, ask yourself the following questions:

- ✦ What really matters most to me in my life? God + Family
- ✦ In what ways can I be replaced—and in what roles am I genuinely irreplaceable? act as a daughter, sister
- ✦ Am I overwhelmed by my schedule? yes
- ✦ Is my health suffering because I have no time to rest? yes
- ✦ Am I spending enough time with those people I love? No
- ✦ When I say yes to something, to what am I saying no? time w God, Reflection, rest

↪ Do I set healthy boundaries around my schedule and commitments? No

When we don't make time for our Prince or for those He has entrusted to our care, we break His heart. And keep in mind that if you don't have time for your kids when they are young, they won't have time for you when you are old. The way we spend our time teaches our children how to spend their time when they are grown.

His Princess Prayer

Dear Lord,

Please take control of my schedule—and convict me, Holy Spirit, about what's on my calendar that is not of kingdom or eternal value. I want to invest wisely my days on this earth. Help me to spend more time with You so I can hear Your voice despite life's busyness. Forgive me, God, for being too busy for what really matters—for living out my love for You and my love for others. I surrender my schedule to You.

Amen.

FREEDOM — EAT AND
EXERCISE TO WIN

Do you not know that in a race all the runners run, but only one gets the prize? Run in such a way as to get the prize. Everyone who competes in the games goes into strict training. They do it to get a crown that will not last; but we do it to get a crown that will last forever.

1 CORINTHIANS 9:24–25, NIV

Something amazing happens inside a woman when she wins victory over her weight and related health issues, and becomes the best version of herself. And that's true for a man as well. When godly Daniel refused to eat the delicacies of the king's table and committed to eat only God's whole-food diet (Genesis 1:29), God blessed him with extra favor, extra wisdom, and extra strength.

Now, I want to tell you that I've spent most of my life searching for a food and exercise plan that I could actually follow and maintain. I feel as if I'm in a neverending war with my weight. Every day I fight against my obsession for the foods that make me tired and overweight. My deep desire is to be fit for my King and healthy enough to complete God's call on my life. Most people look at me and think I'm a commander in chief in this diet war, but I want to confess to you now that my weight is a daily struggle and constant battle for me.

I am a former food addict, and my idea of cutting calories is to stop licking the plate! I've been sixty pounds overweight—and I've won the crown of Mrs. United States of America. I have been the fat girl in high school who never had a prom date—and I have appeared on the cover of a fitness magazine. But no matter what season I'm in regarding my health and weight, a secret fear lurks inside of me, and that is my fear that I may never really win this battle of mind over body. I want the same things any woman wants, to win this diet war once and for all and to be free from having food control me.

I've been speaking at women's conferences for more than ten years, on a wide range of topics. When I speak on the topic of health and weight loss, the audience is full of women who long for help and healing in this area. As a matter of fact, 90 percent of all prayer requests in most churches are for physical healing. You see, there is much more to our weight loss than our appearance. When we are overweight we are much more prone to diseases and health problems, which can cut our call on earth short.

We are royalty and we are called to honor our King with our bodies. This does not mean we need to become "Barbies with Bibles." I will never again be as thin as I was as Mrs. USA. I am over forty and I had a baby late in life and to be honest with you, I'm not willing to work out two hours a day to perfect my body. However, I *am* willing to practice self-control and to get in twenty minutes a day of exercise to clear my mind and maintain my health. I know the battle to lose weight and be healthy is very real, but I believe it can be won!

Wherever your treasure is, there your heart and thoughts will also be.

MATTHEW 6:21, NLT

Our bodies are temples of God's Holy Spirit, and it is time for us to learn to treasure those temples. The Spirit of the living God has chosen our bodies as His dwelling place. He desires that we, the King's princesses, would honor Him with our bodies.

Don't you know that you yourselves are God's temple
and that God's Spirit lives in you?

1 CORINTHIANS 3:16, NIV

If we were to be brutally honest with ourselves, we would probably have to admit that most of our efforts to lose weight have been motivated by a desire to glorify ourselves. Rarely, if ever, do we look at a weight-loss plan and think of our Lord and King and the royal call He has on our lives. If you think about it, most of us will do whatever it takes to attract a man or look good at a reunion or wedding. We will also lose weight to win people's approval and get their attention. But why can't we approach our diets primarily as a way of honoring the One who created our bodies? The truth is, we are more effective in our witness to the world when we feel healthy and are in control of our diets.

Before I became a Christian, I lost sixty pounds in order to compete for a worldly crown. All I ever thought about was me, and the scale dictated my day. I was willing to go without any food I craved and to spend countless hours exercising so I could look my best. I spent five intense years training, and I was totally committed to getting what I wanted more than anything…a national crown awarded by man. When I finally won that crown, most would think "mission accomplished." However, as I look back on those years, I realize the reason I could never stay fit for life: My heart was selfish, my goals were all about me, and I was striving after those goals in my own strength, which is not a lot of strength in the face of life's temptations. The only thing I learned from that time in my life was to be self-absorbed, and I got pretty good at it.

Now maybe you have never wanted to win a beauty crown, but I know that every one of us wants to feel special, loved, and approved of. Most of us fight an ongoing battle in our minds about our image. We wish our bodies would look a certain way, we'd like to maintain a certain weight, and none of us likes ourselves when we are controlled by our cravings. In order to win this war with our weight, we need to set our minds on our royal call, not our cravings. Our diets need to be about our desire to honor our King, not about denying ourselves certain foods.

Queen Esther offers us a good example. Her desire to become queen was not about gaining a position in life; it was about her mission to save her people. Esther's crown was never about riches or glory. Her earthly crown had eternal value much greater than she could have ever imagined. If you belong to the Lord, you also have a mission. If you belong to the Lord, your King says in His Word for you to honor Him with your body as a spiritual act of worship (Romans 12:1). He will give you all that you need to be your best—not for your glory, but for His.

God loves us no matter what we eat or how much we weigh. But He knows that we struggle with loving ourselves when we let food make us feel out of control; He knows we struggle with loving ourselves when we are unhealthy and out of control. So right now imagine Him in the room with you. He has wrapped His loving arms around you, He's looking deep into your eyes, and He's saying something like this:

His Princess Love Letter

My princess,

Your body is so special to Me. I carefully created every part of you. You truly are fearfully and wonderfully made. I made you in My image, and I love you. I don't want you to waste another day worrying about what you don't look like or how much you weigh. Come to Me in the morning and let Me be your mirror. Let Me design your diet; let Me be the strength you need to become your healthiest. You don't have to do this alone; I am here to give you all you need to be free and at peace with yourself.

Love, your King, your Identity

Beloved, I pray that all may go well with you and that you may be in good health, as it goes well with your soul.

3 JOHN 1:2, ESV

HIS PRINCESS DIET PLAN FOR VICTORY

1. PRAY... Every morning confess your weakness to God and ask Him to give you the spirit of self-control. The first

step toward a new beginning is confession. God is faithful to cleanse us when we go to Him in confession. Let me lead you in this prayer.

His Princess Prayer

Dear Jesus,

I want to confess my sin to You. Forgive me for not honoring You with my body. I too easily forget that my body is Your dwelling place. I ask You now to search my heart and show me the ways I am defiling Your temple. Change my heart and my motives. I confess I cannot win this war with my weight in my own power. I need You to be my source of strength and to give me wisdom about what to eat. Please give me the fruit of self-control and help me to honor You with my body and crave the foods You designed for me to eat.

In Your name I pray, amen.

Stop for a moment and reflect on what you just prayed. Write down what the Lord revealed to you about yourself.

Maybe He wants you to clean out all the junk food in your kitchen. Maybe your failure to forgive is holding you hostage to food for comfort. Don't move on until you write down what God has shown you.

2. ASK... someone to hold you accountable to a healthy diet and exercise program. Better yet, ask if that person would join you.

3. FAST... Consider making your diet a fast for your King. For thirty days, fast from any white flour, white sugar, or artificial sweeteners.

4. REMOVE... Do not set yourself up to fail. Take control of your kitchen and remove any and all foods that will tempt you to break your thirty-day fast.

5. PREPARE FOR BATTLE... If you will prepare your meals in advance (e.g., cut up raw salad veggies and put them in individual baggies with paper towels to absorb moisture), you will have a much better chance of winning over temptation. If you want more helpful ideas, visit my website, www.hisprincess.com.

6. PURPOSE... to honor your body as the temple of the Holy Spirit; God will give you the power to prevail. Commit your diet to the Lord, just as Daniel did, then write down your purpose for fasting and display it in a place where you can see it every day.

No food tastes as good as being healthy feels!

FREEDOM—DO WHAT GOD TELLS YOU TO DO

I cannot help you anymore until you do exactly what I have said.
JOSHUA 7:12, CEV

I believe God gets to a point where He says the same thing to us that He said to Joshua:

"I cannot help you anymore, My princess, until you do exactly what I tell you to do."

In Deuteronomy 20, Moses was nearing the end of his life. He had done all that God had asked him to do. He was not perfect, but he was committed to the call God had on his life. Moses had stood up against Pharaoh despite his fears, and he had led his people out of captivity. Moses did his best to get the Israelites to obey the Lord. He wanted them to see God's promises come to pass. But they chose their way over God's way and then spent forty years of their lives wandering aimlessly in the desert.

Choosing their own way led the children of Israel into a new kind of captivity. They missed their crowning moment in life to do something great, to settle in the Promised Land. Today that generation is remembered for their disobedience. Moses tried to warn God's chosen people one more time before he died: God longs to bless you, but receiving His blessings depends on your willingness to obey His commands. If we choose to disobey the Lord, we will not experience the fullness of His blessings. But even worse than that, God will lift His shield of protection from us. Moses then goes on to warn us that curses and diseases will come upon us (Deuteronomy 28:15). Just look around you. There are signs of this truth wherever there is rebellion against God and Christians are living their own way instead of His way. This does not mean God does not love us if we disobey Him—His grace and mercy are with us regardless of our actions.

His love is unconditional . . .

but His promises are not!

We will not experience...

- ✦ peace without trust,
- ✦ power without prayer,
- ✦ victory without accountability,
- ✦ wisdom without reading the Word,
- ✦ health without caring for God's temple (our bodies),
- ✦ blessings without obedience.

Now imagine God personalizing Deuteronomy 30:19 for you: "Today I have given you the choice between life and death, between blessings and curses. I call on heaven and earth to witness the choice you make. Oh, that you would choose life!" (NLT).

Let's take a moment to pray.

His Princess Prayer

Dear Jesus,

I want to be blessed and shielded by Your protection. I confess to You right now that I have done some things my way, and I want to choose Your way today. Show me anything in me that I need to repent of and any situation that I am not handling Your way. I am ready to break through to a blessed life in You. Please lead me by Your Holy Spirit on the path of righteousness and do in me whatever You need to do to prepare me for the work You have for me. I want You to do whatever it takes for me to be in Your perfect will for my life. Today I choose to live life Your way.

In Jesus' name I pray, amen.

I said a prayer like this sixteen years ago, and the Lord showed me that I was living a major area of my life my way: I was handling my relationship with my mom the way I wanted to, not the way He wanted me to.

When I got pregnant with my son, I did not have a

relationship with my mother. My parents divorced when I was thirteen, and I decided to move in with my dad and new stepmother. Of course this choice devastated my mom, and now that I have a daughter, I cannot imagine the loneliness and feelings of rejection my mom must have experienced at that time. She was in much pain from her past, her divorce, her daughter moving out, and her mother rejecting her. She shut down and chose not to have a relationship with me. (When we don't know how to handle pain, I think we go into emotional shock in order to keep ourselves from experiencing any more pain.)

Now I was grown up and going to have a baby of my own, and even though my stepmother was very good for me (she helped me get off drugs, lose weight, and improve my life overall), I sensed the Lord prompting me to reconcile with my birth mom. I wrote her a letter telling her that she was going to be a grandma, and I asked if she could come visit when the baby arrived. A few weeks later I received a box in the mail from her. I thought it was a baby gift, and I could not wait to open it. To my surprise it was a collection of my baby things—shoes, photos, and my birth certificate with a note attached that read, "I wish you had never been born. No one has ever caused me so much pain!"

Before you start judging my mom, know that she was not a horrible person; she was a hurting person who had not yet been healed by the Lord. I understand all that now, but I didn't understand that at the time. My emotional pain was so great that I fell to the floor, curled up in a fetal position, and cried out to God: "Why do I have to suffer for my parents' sin? It wasn't my fault that they divorced. It wasn't my fault that I was forced to choose to live with only one of them. I don't think I did anything wrong!" Then the Lord whispered in my spirit: "Neither did I, but I still went to the cross for you." As I cried a bucket of tears, I obeyed my Lord and wrote a letter to my mom asking her to forgive me for anything I had done to hurt her. I didn't mention how she had hurt me. I will not judge my mother for what she was not. I know that she did the best she could under horrible family circumstances.

Today I love my mom. Today my mom is a born-again Christian. Today my mom lives near me and is a wonderful grandma. And my daughter will never know the broken woman who raised me because her past is where my past is... at the Cross!

Whoever finds his life will lose it,
and whoever loses his life for my sake will find it.

MATTHEW 10:39, NIV

Many people are affected by whether or not we decide to obey God and choose life. I chose life when I obeyed God's command to reconcile with my mother, and my sixteen-year-old son, Jake, has witnessed the healing first-hand. My mom now has the opportunity to love my daughter the way she wanted to love me when I was a child. I am free from the enemy of unforgiveness and I am the loving mom I desire to be. When we do what our God asks us to do, we change. Our lives and the lives of those around us change. God Himself promised that, if we love Him and obey Him, He will bless generation after generation (Genesis 17:7, NIV).

Take a moment to reflect on your own life. Are you struggling with a past relationship that maybe the Lord is prompting you to reconcile? Or is something still, after many years, so painful inside your heart that you are wondering if you can walk through it for healing? For your freedom's sake, I want you to imagine your Savior addressing this next letter to you personally...

His Princess Love Letter

My Princess... Triumph Through Trials

I see you when you are in the garden of grief, My princess. I hear your cry for help in the dark hours of the night. I Myself cried out in the garden the night I was betrayed. I asked My Father for another way, a less painful way. Yet I trusted His will and purpose for My life, and I knew that ultimate victory would come at the cross. So, just as olives must be crushed to make oil, I poured out My life as a love offering for you. Don't ever doubt that I am with you and that I long to take you to a place of comfort, peace, and victory. Even when you cannot see Me from where you are, I am working on your behalf. Give to Me the overwhelming weight of your circumstances and come to Me in prayer. When it is time to leave the garden, I will walk with you across the valley and straight to the cross— where I will transform your trials into triumph.

Love, your Savior and your Victor

*For when your faith is tested, your endurance has a chance to grow.
So let it grow, for when your endurance is fully developed,
you will be strong in character and ready for anything.*

JAMES 1:3-4, NLT

If you are feeling like the Lord is telling you to do something now, take a moment to write down His still small voice of instructions, or else when the darkness comes you will doubt what God is revealing to you in His light. I know that sometimes God's way does not look like the path to victory. But King Solomon warned us in Proverbs that there is a way that seems right to man (to us!), but in the end it leads to destruction (Proverbs 14:12). Know that if we're going to know freedom in Christ, we are going to have to do exactly what God asks us to do no matter how strange His instructions seem.

Think about some Old Testament battle plans. Our King had some unique ideas about how to give victory to His chosen ones. For example, He told Gideon to send home almost all his army before he went to war against a sea of enemies ready to destroy Israel. Gideon obeyed and then stood on the battlefield with just three hundred men who were armed not with swords but with only torches and trumpets. They had listened to and obeyed their King's commands. Not only did Gideon's army win the battle, but not one of the three hundred men died. And they had the privilege of watching their God at work in their personal war. Let's learn from Gideon. Too many times we risk destroying our life by doing what we think is right instead of doing what God knows is right.

So, like Gideon, don't follow anyone into battle except your Lord. He gave His very life for you; clearly He has earned the right to lead you. And, as another Old Testament example shows us, if you follow human advice rather than God's Word, you may end up like the Israelites: wandering in the desert. Like them, you will miss many of the blessings God has for you.

Remember what happened when Moses sent twelve men into Canaan to check out the giants that Israel would have to fight to take over their promised land (Numbers 13:17–31)? Ten of the spies came back and said, "There's no way can we win!" Two of the spies took God at His word and said, "We can win!" Sadly, the Israelites acted on man's discouraging words rather than God's proven, powerful word, and they missed out on blessings God had set them free to enjoy.

"*Be strong and courageous!*
Do not be afraid of them!
The LORD *your God will go ahead of you.*
He will neither fail you nor forsake you."

DEUTERONOMY 31:6, NLT

FREEDOM—OPEN THE GIFT YOUR KING HAS PLACED INSIDE YOU

Each of you has been blessed with one of God's many wonderful
gifts to be used in the service of others. So use your gift well.

1 PETER 4:10, CEV

To win victory, it is important to be in the proper position on the battlefield. God created you with a gift that He wants you to give to the world. The day you received your new life in Christ, that gift was awakened and empowered by the Holy Spirit for use in God's kingdom. That gift is something you love to do, something that energizes and gives you joy, the place where you belong in battle.

If the Lord sent you a personal letter about your gift, it might read like this…

HIS PRINCESS LOVE LETTER

My precious princess,

I have given you the gift of eternal life, but My giving does not stop there. Inside of you is a supernatural surprise—a gift waiting for you to unwrap. Yes, it's there, My love. It's hidden within dreams waiting to be pursued, but it's also swallowed up by daily distractions and drowned out by life's disappointments and uncertainties. Come ask Me about it, My daughter, and I will show you how to unwrap what I placed inside of you before the day you were born. You will find your gift in the place that brings you the greatest joy and in the work you most love to do. Using your gift will satisfy your soul, but this gift is not just for you. I have placed it in you to give away while you shine on earth for me. Don't waste another day trying to be someone you were not created to be. Instead ask Me now, and I will reveal to you who you really are and what you are destined to do for My kingdom.

Love, your King, who longs to see you open your gift

Remember dreaming about what we would be when we grew up? We were sure we could be anything we wanted to be. What happened to that confidence? How did we grow from being a little girl who could do anything to a woman who feels so unsure of herself?

Maybe we started looking to other people to validate who we are. If we're ever going to become all God has gifted us to be then we are going to have to let the Lord tell us who we are, what we are worth, and what He wants us to do to fight the good fight, as the apostle Paul would say. We can't listen to the voices of the world. Let me give you an example.

When I was in high school, an English teacher told me—in front of all my classmates—that I was born to lose in life. From that day on I hated school, and that teacher's words became my identity for years. I never did go to college, and I long believed I would never do anything in life.

But God Himself intervened and changed that wrong belief about myself, and He did so unexpectedly and rather dramatically. Remember the dinner party I told you about? Remember the comment, "I heard you were Jewish, fat, and on drugs. How did you ever become a Christian?" That night as my husband and I were driving home, I felt so ashamed. I was grateful for all that the Lord had done in my life, but that woman had really embarrassed me. But more was happening in that situation than I realized.

That night my King began unwrapping the gift He had placed inside of me. And just a few weeks later that same loud lady called me and asked if I would share my testimony with a large number of Christian leaders. Today I am a full-time speaker, and there is nothing I love more than talking to people about Jesus. I always knew I had a deep passion for communicating with people; I had never recognized that passion as a God-given gift.

We all have an ability that comes naturally, that makes us come alive inside. And something wonderful happens inside of us when we discover what we are destined to do for the glory of the King!

Take a moment to pray this prayer...

His Princess Prayer

Dear God,
I want my life to be a gift to others. I need You to help me overcome my insecurities. I want You to unwrap the person You created me to be. Help me stop trying to win the approval of other people, when I already have Yours.
In Jesus' name I pray, amen.

Your King wants you to live with passion and purpose. He wants you to be at total peace about who you are and what you are here on earth to do. So think for a moment about what truly energizes you and gets you excited. I pray that you don't waste another day not opening your gift or trying to open a gift that doesn't have your name on it. (Can you imagine, on Christmas morning, opening all the gifts that don't belong to you or, even worse, watching everyone enjoying their gifts while you hesitate to even open yours?)

Our Savior died on a cross to give us the gift of eternal life, but our God did not let His only Son stay on that brutal instrument of death. God resurrected Jesus from the dead and raised Him to a place of power so that we may live life abundantly. Such abundant living comes, in part, when you open that special gift inside of you and give it to the world. You are the King's princess, and your gift is part of His eternal plan. Don't waste your life trying to fit into a "gift box" that feels too big or too small. Your God-given gift perfectly fits your personality and is your purpose and position to win victory.

Take a moment to try to identify your gift by asking yourself the following questions.

What do I love to do? *Be with my family*

What makes me come alive inside?

Do I love to…

- ❧ Play a musical instrument
- ❧ Create fine art
- ❧ Make arts and crafts
- ❧ Serve others
- ❧ Sing in a group or solo
- ❧ Perform drama
- ❧ Teach
- ❧ Coordinate events
- ❧ Spearhead projects
- ❧ Listen to people
- ❧ Counsel hurting people
- ❧ Mentor young women
- ❧ Host people in my home
- ❧ Help with organization
- ❧ Work with young children
- ❧ Spend time with teens
- ❧ Volunteer for charities
- ❧ Raise money for ministries
- ❧ Something else: _____

*We have different gifts, according to the grace given us.
If a man's gift is prophesying, let him use it in proportion to his faith.
If it is serving, let him serve; if it is teaching, let him teach;
if it is encouraging, let him encourage;
if it is contributing to the needs of others, let him give generously;
if it is leadership, let him govern diligently;
if it is showing mercy, let him do it cheerfully.*

ROMANS 12:6–8, NIV

God's Word teaches that we all have different gifts.
However, we are all part of one spiritual body. Therefore
every part—every one of us—needs to do our job if we are
to be a healthy church. We also have to stop comparing ourselves to other members of the body, and be careful not to
judge others for what they are not. We are all serving the
same King, but with different functions.

*Just as each of us has one body with many members,
and these members do not all have the same function,
so in Christ we who are many form one body,
and each member belongs to all the others.*

ROMANS 12:4–5, NIV

If we were on an actual battlefield fighting a physical war, winning would depend in large part on each of us doing what we were trained to do. Can you imagine putting someone on the front lines who didn't know how to use a gun? Or what about letting fellow soldiers rather than doctors perform surgeries on the wounded?

We aren't able to see the weapons used against us in the spiritual realm, but God warns us that they are there. The most effective way we can fight the fight—and complete the royal call on our lives—is to use the gifts God has given each of us individually as well as a whole unit.

HIS PRINCESS GIFTS

Princess Prophet

If you have the gift of prophecy, then you are naturally strong in your convictions. You can give us courage to stand for righteousness and lead us to victory as you boldly stand up against the enemy of our souls by exposing sin. You are an excellent example of what it means to fear God more than man.

Princess Server

If you have the gift of service, you naturally see needs the rest of us don't see. You know how to take care of others, and you find and spread joy in helping make caring things happen. You are an excellent example of how Jesus wants us to serve one another.

Princess Teacher

If you have the gift of teaching, you are the watchdog of the Christian army. You can discern truth, you can teach us, and you can help us better understand the King's truth. We could not survive the battle without you. We could not obey our King's commands if you did not teach us how to get right with God. You are an excellent example of how to live with deep conviction in our hearts.

Princess Encourager

If you have the gift of encouragement, you are our spiritual cheerleader. We need you especially when someone or something has wounded us. You help us keep fighting the good fight, you remind us of the King's eternal truths, and you help us soar to new heights in life in Him. You are an excellent example of how to build each other up in our faith.

Princess Giver

If you have the gift of giving, you help supply our spiritual and practical needs. You also teach us to be generous, and you help us discover the true joy of giving. Your gift is behind far-reaching and life-changing charitable organizations, and you have a great desire to see God's kingdom advance. You are an excellent example of what it means to invest in eternity.

Princess Leader
If you have the gift of leadership, you get things done; you make things happen. Without you, we would not have retreats, conventions, or order in the church. You see the big picture, you know how to direct people where they can best serve, and you help dreams become reality. You are an excellent example of what it means to put our purpose into action.

Princess Mercy
If you have the gift of mercy, you are part of the nerve system of the body of Christ. You feel our pain, you share our burdens, you listen to us with your whole heart, and you show us how to serve others deeply. When you share your gift, you show us God's mercy, and you help us get through life's tough times. You are an excellent example of how to show God's tenderness to the world.

I pray that you have found your gift—and may you use it to bless others rather than impress others. And may you never again doubt that you are called for a kingdom purpose.

FREEDOM—MOVE ON FROM THE PAST

"Forget the former things;
do not dwell on the past.
See, I am doing a new thing!"
ISAIAH 43:18–19, NIV

I know from my painful past that this verse is easer said than done. It is hard to "forget the former things" and truly believe that God is "doing a new thing" in our hearts and in our lives. We need to remember that our past remains in our memory to teach us, not to torment us.

If the Lord wrote you this Scripture in a love letter, it would read like this:

HIS PRINCESS LOVE LETTER

My princess,

Forget the former things! All have sinned and fallen short of My glory. If you've confessed your sins, I've forgiven them, so move on! I gave My life so you could be free from your past and live a new life in Me. Forgive those who have hurt you, and most important, forgive yourself. There is no wrong great enough to keep Me from redeeming you. Read My Word, My love. All My chosen ones have made mistakes and have gone through trials. I was with them, and I am with you today. I am ready to do a new thing in you, so trust Me to work out the things that have gone wrong in the past. It's time for you to move forward and do what I sent you here to do.

Love, your Savior, Jesus

OUR KING IN ACTION

Shadrach, Meshach, and Abed-nego, three men deeply committed to God, were put into a blazing-hot furnace because they loved God and obeyed Him even when doing so ran counter to civil law. Human wisdom predicted that these men would burn to death, but God had a bigger plan. Not only did the men survive the fire, but they didn't even smell like smoke when the guards lifted them out of the flames.

Something beautiful happens inside of us after we come out of life's wildfire: We become purified in the fire. We appreciate life in a deeper way. Our faith in God becomes stronger, and our endurance for the journey of faith increases.

When a silversmith puts his precious metal in a fire, he never takes his eyes off of it, and he does not remove it until he can see his own reflection in it. Likewise, our King is more concerned about our character than about our comfort, so He will let us remain in the fire until He sees His own reflection in us. After all, it is a Christlike character that will give us the endurance to win this spiritual war against the enemy of our soul. And with a Christlike character we will impact future generations for God's kingdom.

*When your faith is tested, your endurance has a chance to grow.
So let it grow, for when your endurance is fully developed,
you will be strong in character and ready for anything.*

JAMES 1:3–4, NLT

Redeemed by God, our pain can give us the drive to complete our purpose. Remember the English teacher who told me I was born to lose? Twenty years after she made that remark, I was invited to speak at two conventions to a total of thirteen thousand California teachers. Again, all I could think about when I received that invitation was how unqualified I was to address such a large group of educators. I was sure that if one English teacher didn't like me, then all teachers would feel the same about me.

I will never forget sitting on that stage in Sacramento waiting anxiously to speak. I held a paper bag to breathe into so I wouldn't pass out from hyperventilation. As I looked out at the sea of teachers, I heard a voice in my head whispering, *You were born to lose.* But I turned my fear into a prayer, and the Lord reminded me that I had been in that very convention center before....

The last time I had been in that building, I was high on drugs, worshiping an acid-rock band, and singing about the devil. At the very moment I flashed on that memory, I was called up to speak. I walked to the podium and stood there not as I used to be, but as who I had become in Christ. I shared with a grateful heart what God had done for me, and I spoke in God-confidence—not mine. I encouraged the teachers to remember how greatly they influence our future generation. I reminded them that they are educating our future leaders. When I finished speaking, I received a standing ovation from the people I had most feared—teachers!

It was at that speaking engagement that I realized God used my English teacher to teach me His rule of punctuation: Don't put a period in your life where God has a comma. God has a plan for every person He creates. He has an amazing plan for you personally, and He will complete it if you will give Him your pain, your problems, and the people who have hurt you—because your Daddy in heaven knows how to place you in a royal position regardless of who has tried to keep His purpose for your life from being accomplished. That English teacher wanted me to put a period on my life; God definitely didn't!

"For I know the plans I have for you," declares the LORD,
"plans to prosper you and not to harm you,
plans to give you hope and a future."

JEREMIAH 29:11, NIV

Don't put a period in your life

where God has a comma.

His Princess Prayer for You

I pray that you will leave your past where it belongs: at the Cross, to be forgiven and redeemed by Jesus. I also pray that you will focus on living out your God-given, royal purpose in this life. Our King is waiting for us to say, "Yes, Lord! I will represent You to the world." Regardless of where we have been or what we have done, God can and will use us for His kingdom.

In Jesus' name I pray this for you, amen.

THE APOSTLE PETER…had to MOVE ON and let go of his guilt. He had denied Jesus three times, but if he had hung onto that guilt, he would not have fulfilled his call as the King's apostle. He also would not have contributed to the holy Scriptures that we read today.

QUEEN ESTHER…had to MOVE ON from her identity as a powerless orphan and accept God's call to be queen. If she had focused on how unqualified she was to reign, she would have missed the opportunity to save the Jewish people and be a part of God's great eternal plan for His chosen ones.

KING DAVID...had to MOVE ON from his sins of adultery and murder. He cried out to God and received His forgiveness. God is so full of grace that He made something good out of David's bad choice by giving him and Bathsheba King Solomon once they repented and moved on.

THE APOSTLE PAUL...had to MOVE ON from being a pompous persecutor of Christians and embrace his calling to serve Jesus, the Savior and Lord of the very people he had persecuted. If Paul had not left behind his past, the New Testament would be much shorter, and we would be without his bold and passionate example of living a life devoted to Christ.

We are called to be God's princesses, and He frees us to serve Him and reign with Him by the power of His grace, His mercy, and His forgiveness. We are new creations because He loved us with His very life. Amen!

His Princess Prayer

Lord,

Your Word tells me that I am a new creation, that I am not the same person I was before I met You, and that the old me is gone. I desperately want to believe that, but I need Your help. Please show me how to live as the new person You have created me to be. Renew my mind, my spirit, and my image of myself. Please show me the things I need to do to represent You well. Make me as white as snow and give me a heart for eternity. I choose this day to believe that You will complete me in every way.

In Jesus' name I pray, amen.

Take a moment and review the King's battle plan for **FREEDOM** once more:

Find the root of the pain or problem
Run to God
Edit your life
Eat and exercise to win
Do what God tells you to do
Open the gift your King has placed inside you
Move on from the past

Applying this freedom plan to your life is key to reigning in victory with your King. True freedom is worth fighting for, so fight the good fight—in His power! Then you will know total victory—and that means living with purpose in your heart, peace in your mind, and the power to do great things. That is the only way His princess should live!

Blessed is the man [or woman] who perseveres under trial, because when he has stood the test, he will receive the crown of life that God has promised to those who love him.

JAMES 1:12, NIV

three

Royal Relationships

THE ART OF LOVING
ONE ANOTHER

hat makes our hearts melt when we sit in the theater and watch a great love story? It's not the hero's physical strength or his beloved's beauty. You and I are drawn to the power of true love and its inexplicable ability to prevail despite tragedy and hardship. Often, the greater the conflict, the greater the love.

A problem comes, though, when we get accustomed to seeing relational problems solved in the time it takes to eat a bag of popcorn and drink a soda. Our hero and his beauty have less than two hours to defeat the dragons and overcome unspeakable challenges (and even less if we're watching a situation comedy on TV, where relational conflicts magically resolve themselves in less than thirty minutes). You and I are not going to magically resolve any relationship in our own wisdom, and definitely not in less than two hours. However, the Author of love, our Prince of Peace, has written a script. His Word on real-life royal relationships can lead us to the happy ending we long for!

A few years ago, I was on a late-night cross-country plane trip with my husband. The flight was smooth, the lights were low, and the hum of the engines had lulled most of the passengers to sleep. "Will you dance with me?" my husband whispered. How could I resist a spontaneous moment of romance?

Moments later we were at the back of the plane—holding each other close and dancing to our own music at forty thousand feet. We were in our own little world when a flight attendant tapped my husband on the shoulder.

"I'm sorry to interrupt your romantic moment, but... well... we have a bet going with our crew that you two are having an affair."

"Well... you caught us," my husband replied. "This is my bride of fifteen years... and we try to have an 'affair' like this whenever we can."

The flight attendant began to laugh, but moments later

another one of them approached us with tears in her eyes.

"You have no idea how desperately I needed to see that you two love each other. I was going to file for divorce this week!"

The world needs to see Christian husbands and wives love each other. Our children, our friends, and even perfect strangers are secretly desperate to see if real love is possible in this world of betrayal and pain. They need hope that love can be rekindled, that fruit can grow from a dying tree.

That romantic moment with my husband was the fruit of much nurturing—of desperately fighting for—our relationship. And it came after many tears and much wrestling with the painful truth that our marriage was far from perfect. It took everything in us to get beyond our differences, to stay married, and to learn the art of truly loving one another. The tragedy is that many of us married couples give up too soon and never do taste the sweetness of a late-night dance.

"It is not good for the man to be alone."
GENESIS 2:18, NIV

At every step of His creative efforts, God pronounced His handiwork "good." Isn't it interesting that the first thing that *wasn't* good, in God's estimation, was Adam standing alone in the Garden? "It is not good for the man to be alone"—and this verse in Genesis isn't just about marriage. This verse is about relationships. God made us relational—to need one another, to experience the true joy of relationship.

Someone once asked Mother Teresa what the worst disease facing mankind is. This tiny woman had spent her life in sacrificial service, ministering in Calcutta to the sick and the dying, one precious soul at a time. According to Mother Teresa, the greatest disease is *loneliness*, and tragically, it is more rampant in Western civilizations like the United States than anywhere else in the world. Maybe our comforts and conveniences are getting in the way of the very thing we need most…one another.

> *Two people can accomplish more than twice as much as one;*
> *they get a better return for their labor.*
> *If one person falls, the other can reach out and help.*
> *But people who are alone when they fall are in real trouble.*
> ECCLESIASTES 4:9–10, NLT

Loneliness, like cancer, may not manifest any symptoms at first. We suffer on the inside but appear to be fine on the outside. We smile to people at work, we sing in the pew at church, and we do a good job keeping our "life is great and I'm happy" look on our face. Yet, if we were really honest with ourselves, many of us would say, "I feel so alone."

Why do we suffer in quiet, lonely desperation?

1. Maybe we don't want to appear weak or needy.

So we choose to stay isolated; we create an image that says, "I am secure on my own." The enemy of our soul loves it when we do this. In fact, he tries to separate us from other people. That is one of his most important and often unrecognized strategies. When a lion is hungry, the king of beasts doesn't go after the whole herd. He can't defeat a herd, and he doesn't even try. Instead, he goes after an isolated animal. Likewise, the devil tries to separate an unsuspecting victim from the body of believers. His goal is to isolate the weak, and he sees past the painted smile on our face. We might as well paint a bull's-eye on our chest and say, "Come and get me, Satan! I'm alone."

2. Maybe we are afraid of getting hurt or being rejected.

So we convince ourselves that we don't need anybody. We ignore the voice inside of us screaming, "Somebody love me!" Many of us don't know how to give love or receive love, so we close the door of our hearts and isolate ourselves from the true Source of life and love. We separate ourselves from the herd and, to mix metaphors, become like a pond in the wilderness. No fresh water comes in, no water leaves, and we become stagnant. Eventually our isolation becomes unhealthy for us and for those who need us—and that isolation can become deadly.

Wherever the river flows, life will flourish.
EZEKIEL 47:9, THE MESSAGE

Then the angel showed me the river of the water of life, as clear as crystal, flowing from the throne of God and of the Lamb.
REVELATION 22:1, NIV

#3. *Maybe we are not willing to be open and honest.*
We find ourselves drawn to movies about intense, intimate relationships, and we love happy endings. But intimacy doesn't come easily in real life, and happy endings aren't neatly scripted. (By the way, when real-life happy endings come—and they do—they would not be nearly as meaningful if the relationship had not been fought for.)

Like the scriptwriter for a movie, our King has written for us the greatest love story of all. It tells about how He loved us with His life, and we are to follow His example and give of ourselves. Nothing will draw you closer to someone than giving yourself to him or her. If we stop trying to impress one another and instead begin to bless one another, we will begin to experience the true joy of friendship. Loneliness is often rooted in selfishness or the fear of getting hurt. It is truly beautiful to watch people who have learned the art of loving one another.

#4. *Many times we enter relationships only for what we can get out of them.*
And we end up getting nothing of real value. Selfish relationships always end in heartache and disappointment. But when we enter a relationship concerned about what we can give, we receive more than we ever imagined.

Take a moment to reflect on a time that God used you to refresh another person or relieve someone's burden. You felt great inside; you felt as if your life mattered. You also felt closer to that person, and that person felt closer to you.

King Solomon observed:

> *Those who refresh others will themselves be refreshed.*
> PROVERBS 11:25, NLT

Despite these four barriers, I believe we can master the art of royal relationships and enrich our lives forever. Many of us have simply never been taught how to have a healthy relationship. Like me, many of you come from broken homes, or you've been in relationships that have caused great pain. Relationships can be the source of our greatest joy or the cause of our deepest disappointment and pain. But God can heal and redeem those hurts, and we can know the joy of intimacy with other people.

Let's look now at God's Word and discover His "Ecclesiastes 4:12 wisdom" about relationships...

> *A person standing alone can be attacked and defeated,*
> *but two can stand back-to-back and conquer.*
> *Three are even better,*
> *for a triple-braided cord is not easily broken.*
> ECCLESIASTES 4:12, NLT

We all know there is no such thing as a perfect relationship, because we are all imperfect human beings; but there *is* an art to loving one another. When by God's grace and instruction you master this art, you will become very rich in relationships.

If you are ready to find out how well you are doing in the art of relationships, ask yourself—and those people closest to you—this question: "How do others feel about themselves after they have spent time with me?"

Do they feel…?

- ⬦ Drained
- ⬦ Jealous
- ⬦ Depressed
- ⬦ Envious
- ⬦ Hurt
- ⬦ Inferior
- ⬦ Overwhelmed
- ⬦ Used
- ⬦ Unaccepted

Do they feel…?

- ⬦ Loved
- ⬦ Safe
- ⬦ Motivated
- ⬦ Encouraged
- ⬦ Accepted
- ⬦ Appreciated
- ⬦ Refreshed
- ⬦ Cared for
- ⬦ Affirmed

Do for others what you would like them to do for you.
This is a summary of all that is taught in the law and the prophets.
MATTHEW 7:12, NLT

The ultimate example of a real-life royal relationship in the Bible is the remarkable friendship between King David and Jonathan.

Jonathan was King Saul's son and next in line for the throne of Israel. But God had anointed David to be the next king, and He was allowing a fiercely jealous Saul to try to kill the younger warrior. None of these circumstances, however, could destroy David and Jonathan's friendship.

Once, while a lonely and discouraged David was hiding in a dark cave, Jonathan visited him. Dressed in his royal garments, Jonathan did not intend to exalt himself in front of David. He was not wearing his royal wardrobe to brag or boast, but in order to symbolically strip himself of his right to the throne by giving David all that he was wearing. Jonathan's beautiful act of love and honor gave David back his hope of one day ruling as God had said he would.

Jonathan loved David so deeply that he gave up his legal and personal rights and bowed to God's will. At that moment, the Bible says, their souls were knit together. If you think about it, this relationship could have taken many wrong turns.

- A self-centered and self-exalting Jonathan could have taken great joy in the fact that his father was trying to kill David.
- David could have rejected Jonathan's friendship because he was Saul's son and Saul wanted him dead.
- Jonathan could have walked away from David in his dark hours of waiting on the Lord's timing for his ascension to the throne.

The beauty of this royal relationship is that Jonathan and David did not let the dark spirit of jealousy, disappointment, discouragement, pride, or family ties destroy their God-ordained friendship. And that's a key point: Royal relationships happen when we care more about God's will for one another than about our rights. And the tough times—the times that call for sacrifice—give us the opportunity to prove that we are real friends. Anyone can hang in there when all is going well!

Let's pray...

His Princess Prayer

Dear God,

I confess that I have not had the right heart to have royal relationships. Please forgive me for my selfish motives...and remove my fear of getting hurt. Teach me how to have more joy from giving than receiving...and show me how to be the type of friend I desire to have. Open my eyes that I may see people as You do, and give me the heart to love others the way You do.

In Jesus' name I pray, amen.

CARING FOR EACH OTHER

Do not withhold good from those who deserve it when it's in your power to help them.

PROVERBS 3:27, NLT

God commands us not to withhold good when we are able to help those who are in need. Too often, though, we do all we can for those who don't need our acts of service. When we do this, we burn ourselves out and become bitter toward those who don't appreciate our expression of love. There are two reasons we displace our love like this, and both of them are rooted in self, not in selfless, generous love or the blessing of true friendship.

#1. *Caring in order to gain approval or a sense of worth.*
If we spend our entire life caring and serving others in an attempt to validate our worth, the enemy of our soul will put people in our path who use and abuse us. We will always get hurt when we give out of such selfish motives. Furthermore, we will see no fruit from those friendships because our hearts won't be in a place for receiving love.

Giving of ourselves is useless if our motive is to bring glory to anyone other than our King. Besides, no one will ever see you or love you as Jesus does, and no one can reward you for your acts of love as He can and will.

If you see yourself in the above description, then I invite you to pray this prayer:

His Princess Prayer

Dear Jesus,

I confess that I am desperate for others to love me and approve of me. I have wasted a lot of time doing for others so that I will feel good about myself. Please release me now from giving people the power to define my value. Please teach me to look to You to validate my worth. Carve in my memory the price You paid for me the day You died on that cross. Let Your life and love for me be all that I need.

In Your name I pray, amen.

#2. *Caring in order to get others to love us.*

Caring for others makes for close relationships, but our motive for caring cannot be that of getting someone to love us. That is not the road toward a relationship that nurtures and grows us. And if we choose that road, the enemy will put people in our path that will treat us like slaves starved for affection. Think about those relationships where you can never measure up to the other people's expectations, and the more you try to, the more they reject you. You either become obsessed with trying to get them to love you, or you start playing their games and pretending that you don't care or doing things to make them feel the pain you feel. These approaches are not God's plan for relationships; they are mind games that nobody wins. If you are playing relational Battleship with someone—whether men, parents, or girlfriends—you will not win the love you're after.

If this description reminds you of yourself, I invite you to pray with me for strength and courage to stop playing these destructive games forever.

His Princess Prayer

Dear God,

I confess I have allowed others to play dangerous games with my mind and emotions in order to try to win their affection. I ask You to show me where I'm doing that right now in any relationship I'm in. I need You to set me free from my vain efforts to win love; I ask You to free me to feel Your love so that I will be able to love others. Lord, let me know how to walk off the game field and teach me, by Your Holy Spirit, how to have real-life royal relationships.

In Jesus' name I pray, amen.

Genuine Caring

Have you noticed that we all have different ways of expressing love and different ways of feeling loved? That being the case, you and I need to ask our loved ones what makes them feel loved. We may be placing too much effort on the things they don't need from us or things they don't value. But we can take the guessing game out of how to say "I love you." We can learn the love languages of those we love. I'll explain.

Just as real artists study their craft, we need to study the people we love. We need to notice what they like and what they need as they go through different seasons of life. Keep in mind that all relationships go through different seasons. Life never stays the same. At times those you love will need compassion and understanding, at other times they may need a lot of nurturing, and still at other times they may need acts of service from you. So take time to talk about what's going on in each other's lives. Ask, "What can I do to be a blessing to you today?" Then you will truly know how to care for each other and begin to master your relationships throughout the changing seasons of life.

HIS PRINCESS IN ACTION

When I had my first baby, my life changed drastically. I had been single until I was twenty-seven, and all my friends knew me as the "party girl" who was always up for some fun. Then I got married and got pregnant on our honeymoon.

Needless to say, my free and easy life of spontaneity came to a halt. Unfortunately, many of my single friends resented me for no longer being as involved in their worlds. Because of their attitudes, I felt like a failure as a friend.

Then one day a single friend dropped by to see me unexpectedly. When I answered the door at two in the afternoon, exhausted, still wearing my robe, and with my house a total mess, she could see that I was not a flaky friend who had forgotten her. She realized that I was just trying to find my way as a wife and mom. This friend stopped criticizing me and started that day to truly care for me. Instead of giving me reasons to feel guilty, she gave me a day of rest: She watched my baby and completely cleaned my house while I took a six-hour nap. When I woke up, I had a newly clean house, a rested, clear mind—and something even better: I'd had someone truly care for me, and that single day of our friendship meant more than all the years of crazy fun we'd shared when I was single. Something special happens in our relationships when we come to the rescue of a friend in the right way and for the right reasons.

HIS PRINCESS WISDOM

You don't have to burn yourself out running to everyone's rescue. Invest wisely when and where you're truly needed. Royal relationships are rich in love, not because of the amount of time spent together, but because of perfect timing and the perfect touch.

Due to our busy lives and the different seasons we were in, I didn't see that friend often after that special day. But ever since then, when we did get together, we were instantly connected. She had taken the time to care for me in a way I needed when I needed it most. She did what this verse from Proverbs says: "Do not withhold good...when it's in your power to help" (Proverbs 3:27, NLT). In my opinion, the mark of a true friendship is when you come in contact after a long separation and can pick up right where you left off, just as if no time had gone by.

Cover One Another's Offenses

He who covers over an offense promotes love,
but whoever repeats the matter separates close friends.
PROVERBS 17:9, NIV

These words offer a wealth of wisdom about the art of loving one another. We all find ourselves tempted to repeat a juicy matter of interest (also known as gossip!), but if we are going to have the deep, meaningful relationships we long for, then we are going to have to choose to cover our friends' frailties and loved ones' mistakes by keeping details about their personal lives to ourselves. No one benefits when we expose one another's weaknesses to other people. In fact, everyone loses.

I've learned the hard way that it takes a lot more character to cover over someone's sins and failings than it does to expose them. Remember that the enemy's mission is to keep us from being close to one another. If we aren't careful with our words, we will actually be helping him separate us from one another. When people share a deeply personal part of their life with you, they are giving you the great privilege of allowing you into their private world. They are saying that they trust and value you enough to share secrets of their heart. When we understand this truth about trust, we will want to treasure and protect the things we know about one another rather than expose them for everyone to see.

HIS PRINCESS IN ACTION

I have a dear friend who knows every deep, dark secret of my life, and we are knit together like David and Jonathan. Because she is the one person who keeps my secrets as a treasure in her heart, she is my safe place. When we first met several years ago, she lived in California and I lived in Arizona. We vacationed together, and we talked on the phone almost every day. But she had never come to stay at my home.

Now, my precious friend is the Martha Stewart of Christian living. No one I've ever met can host a guest better than she does. I loved going to her home. Then, two years into our friendship, she decided to break away from her busy life and come spend a weekend with me. I was very excited about having her all to myself, and I was counting the days until her arrival. But I had never been taught how to host a guest. In fact, at that point in my life, I had never had people stay in my home. So when she walked in the door, she saw a sloppy house, dirty bathrooms, and no food in the fridge. There was nothing that indicated how excited I was that she was there. But rather than criticizing me, she chose to cover over my offenses and share with me, as my mentor, her gift of hospitality.

The next morning she showed me how to be a host. I wrote everything down, and for years I've applied all that she so graciously taught me. Now I fix meals for my guests in advance so I have time to visit with the ones I love, I put gift bags on their very clean guest bed, I warm their robes while they're showering in my clean bathroom, I don't use my phone while I'm with them, and I minister to them with prayer and words of encouragement.

Now, my friend could have reported to the girls' gossip mill what a horrible hostess I had been. She could have cut off our friendship because I did not measure up to her expectations of a hostess. She also could have held bitterness and anger inside all weekend rather than tell me the truth in love and teach me how to be a host.

Close, intimate relationships don't happen without times of disappointment, but our King tells us to do for others what we would have them do for us. So ask yourself in every situation, "If our roles were reversed, what would I want her response to be?"

We need to cover over one another's offenses if we want solid friendships that will last a lifetime.

Sometimes those who are dear to our

hearts need love the most

when they deserve it the least.

His Princess Prayer

Dear God,

Please forgive me for not covering over the offenses of my family and friends, and convict me when I am inadvertently helping the enemy destroy my relationships with them. Teach me to treasure the truth about them that they entrust me. Open my eyes to see the people in my life the way You see them, and enable me to extend to them the same grace that You give to me.

In Jesus' name I pray, amen.

Most important of all, continue to show deep love for each other,
for love covers a multitude of sins.

1 PETER 4:8, NLT

COMMUNICATE WITH ONE ANOTHER

All of us have felt the pain of being misunderstood. It's discouraging to express ourselves in love only to see our words become the very thing that separates us from the one we care about. I think we see this especially in marriage: Rather than draw you closer to your spouse, your words can painfully tear you away from each other. God's Word warns us that the power of life and death is in our tongues; we can heal or hurt someone with a word. The key to mastering the art of communication is remembering just how powerful our words really are.

Also powerful and very damaging is our silence. Communication breaks down if we choose not to communicate at all. Maybe we have shut down, not wanting to be heard or seen or noticed, because we have been put down most of our lives. I know the pain of being put down, but I also know that the Master Artist can take those wounds and use them to turn you into a beautiful, compassionate woman who is careful with her words. The King's healing touch can bring you back to life so you don't have to hide any longer. He loves you and He will do whatever it takes to help you become the princess He wants you to be... but you must go to Him!

His Princess Prayer

Dear God,

Sometimes I am afraid to speak because I'm afraid I'll say the wrong words. Please remove my fear and replace it with faith in You. Fill my heart with Your love and my mouth with Your words. Give the people I'm talking to the ability to know my heart even when my words come out wrong. I thank You for the privilege You have given me to pray, and I trust You to guide my lips to speak words of Your love.

In Jesus' name, amen.

Communication also breaks down when we offer, so to speak, only a black-and-white copy of ourselves rather than the original. No one values what isn't real. But too many of us try so hard to say what we think will make us look good rather than giving the gift of genuineness and transparency. With that effort we close the door to real-life royal relationships.

We've all probably experienced the frustration of a fake friendship when we act like "Barbies with a Bible." Those relationships amount to little more than wasted words and wasted time, and often we become even more plastic as a result of those insincere connections. Barbie looks perfect on the outside, but we all know she is plastic and totally empty on the inside. His princesses are far from empty on the inside. How could they be when the spirit of the living God is in them? It's time to take off our masks and let the Lord reveal Himself through the way we communicate with each other.

Take a moment to think about your relationships. Ask God to show you which relationships are not genuine and which are of real value.

Let's pray...

His Princess Prayer

Dear God,

Help me to communicate in a way that is real. Take off my mask and replace it with Your reflection. Let me be as real as King David was. Set me free from myself and let me speak like royalty—with kindness and respect, with self-control and affirmation. Let every one of my conversations be rich in the traits that matter to You.

In Jesus' name I pray, amen.

Remember that the more open and honest we are with one another, the closer we become. Nothing can separate what God puts together, so let's build relationships that show the world that we are His.

His Princess in Action

I was at a busy restaurant with some pastors' wives, and we were taking turns sharing the great things God has done in our lives through pain and trials. We cried and laughed together as we openly and transparently talked about how hard life can get. The young man waiting on us came to our table at least ten times within that one lunch hour. Even during his break he stayed close enough to listen to our conversation.

When he brought us our bill, he said, "Thank you for sitting in my section. It was a pleasure to hear you talk. I've never experienced such joy in listening to a group of women." I realized at that moment that the world is not only watching us. It's listening too!

What impression does your conversation make on people? That young man, who had nothing in common with us, couldn't help but notice real love in action. God just may use that powerfully in his life.

We've talked about the two things that break down communication—silence and insincerity. Now let's paint a picture of communication that glorifies our King. Let's look at a few other things to avoid.

Think about how to respond to others when they are going through tough times. One of the biggest mistakes we make is telling someone how good we have it compared to their situation.

- ↪ When one of your girlfriends tells you she is struggling in her marriage, it is not the time to paint a picture of how great your husband is.
- ↪ When someone is discouraged about the lack of funds needed to pay the bills, it is not the time to reveal that God is showering you with financial blessings.
- ↪ When a new mother tells you how housebound and exhausted she feels, it is not the time to say how happy you are to be free of diapers and feel rested again.
- ↪ When a couple tells you that their teenager is in total rebellion, it is not a time to talk about your own teenager's amazing accomplishments and early acceptance into college.

Remember the question I told you to ask yourself earlier, "How do others feel about themselves after they have spent time with me?" Most of us want to be a good friend; we want to learn the art of loving others with our words as well as our actions. So take a moment to think about what your words contribute to the lives of others.

Think about how you respond to people in pain. Ask God to give you the ability to share His love and compassion through your words. Even if you cannot relate to someone's particular situation, you can pray for that person and help lift the burden that way. And continue to ask God to teach you the art of speaking words of encouragement and affirmation.

His Princess Prayer

Dear God,

Use my tongue to paint a picture of Your love. Give me the right words—Your words—when someone is sharing deep pain. Forgive me for bragging about the blessings You have given me when others are going through a trial. In those situations, use me to make them feel the way You make me feel—loved, accepted, and encouraged.

In Jesus' name I pray, amen.

CONFRONT ONE ANOTHER

"If another believer sins against you, go privately and point out the fault."
MATTHEW 18:15, NLT

Jesus gives us two specific instructions in this verse: First, we are to "go privately," and second, we are to "point out the fault." If we choose any other way to resolve conflict than God's way, we will never know the blessings of lasting relationships. Sadly, too often we don't follow God's way.

One big mistake we make is going public with the relational conflict rather than going privately to the person involved. Suddenly everyone knows there is a problem except for the person with whom we have a conflict. This course of action leads to total devastation for many reasons.

1. We have broken trust by taking personal issues public; once trust is broken, reconciliation of that relationship is a much greater challenge.
2. We drag people into a situation that is none of their concern and we influence others to think wrongly about them.
3. We are not loving the person we're in conflict with the way we'd want that person to love us. And we certainly aren't glorifying God with our words or actions.

4. We are showing ourselves to be untrustworthy. If we'll make public a conflict with one person, we'll probably do the same again with another person.

5. We are sinning against our Lord by not handling confrontation His way.

In the second part of Matthew 18:15, God gives us permission to point out the fault or offense. He doesn't want us to ignore the hurtful things people say and do; He doesn't want us to keep quiet about the offense. If we choose not to confront the person who has offended us, that offense will be the beginning of a growing wall of bitterness and resentment toward that person. That wall may eventually become so big that neither party involved can scale it, and the relationship will die.

Our human alternatives to God's instruction may seem right or justified—or easier—at the time of the hurt. Our silence might seem spiritual and sacrificial, and telling everyone about the offense may seem right because we're reporting the truth. But the book of Proverbs says it best:

There is a way which seems right to a man and appears straight before him, but at the end of it is the way of death.

PROVERBS 14:12, AMP

The art of royal relationships requires the right colors and clean brushes. None of us can paint a good picture of relationships on a dirty canvas, especially if the only pictures of relationships we know don't reflect God's ways.

His Princess Prayer

Dear God,

Show me any past relationships that I have left unresolved. Forgive me for the times I've exposed people rather than confronting them privately. Forgive me for the times when I've chosen to hide my feelings rather than confront the one who offended me. Whatever the situation and whatever my sin in mishandling it, please help me do what I can to make the relationship right. Give me courage to confront those who have hurt or offended me—and help me to trust You no matter what the outcome of my efforts. Enable me to do the right thing in Your sight.

In Jesus' name I pray, amen.

His Princess in Action

I praise God for people in my past who have been brave enough to risk our relationship to be open and honest with me about ways I offended them. Many times God puts these people in our path for our personal growth even if they don't remain lifetime friends. And not every friend will be a friend for life. Different seasons of life call for relationships with different people, and relationships themselves have their different seasons. Let me share an example.

I went through a season in my marriage when I suffered greatly from loneliness and resentment. I so much wanted to be happily married that I decided to hide from my husband, Steve, whenever he hurt me—and I hid by saying nothing! Many times the men in our lives hurt us without knowing it, but the pain is still very real. But I stayed silent for fear that Steve would not understand me and for fear that I would not live happily ever after. I also wanted to avoid conflict, something I think a lot of us can relate to.

After several years of hiding, I fell completely out of love with Steve. I had built a high and thick wall of unforgiveness and resentment. That wall was huge to me, but it was invisible to Steve, so when he hit it, he could not understand why I was so cold and distant from him. To make matters worse, I was a Christian speaker and Mrs. United States at the time (a title that spoke of marriage). Needless to say, I was paralyzed by my pain and trapped inside that cold wall of loneliness I had built around myself.

One day another man, a friend Steve and I had led to the Lord, found the key to unlock the door of my heart: He listened to me with his heart and he prayed for me. After three months of listening to and sharing my hidden hurts, this man had captured my heart so much that I wanted to leave my marriage and my ministry. Even though we never had a physical affair, we had an affair of the heart. I knew it was a sin, but I could not stop seeing him. Only when I finally cried out to God to rescue me from that dangerous place was I freed from the pull of the relationship. God rescued me by sending godly women and men to confront me privately. These men and women were on my ministry's advisory board, and if they had not had the courage to confront me or the compassion to feel my pain and pray for me, I would not be married or in the ministry today.

Confrontation is just as much of a gift as comforting or caring for one another. If we really love one another, we will fix what is broken in our relationships, and we will keep those we know and love from falling into the temptations or the traps of the enemy. Today I am more than just married; I'm in love with my husband more than I ever dreamed possible. When something is not right, I pray for perfect timing to talk to him, and then I talk to him privately. I have learned not to build any more walls around me because walls do not protect us from pain. All they do is imprison us. We become slaves to self-pity and loneliness.

Walls do not protect us from pain.

All they do is imprison us.

I want to give you two valuable tools to apply to your royal relationships.

Tool #1: Truth

Don't hide your hurts. Be truthful with yourself and with the people with whom you're in relationship. Take time and invest the energy necessary to heal your relationships, and do so privately.

He who covers over an offense promotes love,
but whoever repeats the matter separates close friends.

PROVERBS 17:9, NIV

Tool #2: *Trusted Friends*

Surround yourself with the kind of people you want to be like. This verse in Proverbs says it best:

> *H*e who walks with the wise grows wise,
> but a companion of fools suffers harm.
>
> PROVERBS 13:20, NIV

One more note. Confrontation is not the same as criticism. Confrontation brings restoration, but criticism brings discouragement and pain. If someone in your life is constantly criticizing you, speak up (confront that person!) and ask him or her to stop. If that person continues, then set boundaries in that relationship; limit your contact with that person.

> *D*ear brothers and sisters, if another Christian is overcome by some sin,
> you who are godly should gently and humbly
> help that person back onto the right path.
>
> GALATIANS 6:1, NLT

Counsel One Another

Let the words of Christ, in all their richness,
live in your hearts and make you wise.
Use his words to teach and counsel each other.

COLOSSIANS 3:16, NLT

If we want to master the art of truly royal relationships, we need God's Word to guide us. Just like the artist who desires the highest quality paint and brushes, we need the Creator of life to engrave His Word in our hearts and minds. Then we will become rich in wisdom and valuable as a friend. If you think about it, our words are really worthless if they only reflect our opinion. King Solomon said this:

My child, be warned: There is no end of opinions
ready to be expressed. Studying them can go on forever
and become very exhausting!

ECCLESIASTES 12:12, NLT

People in royal relationships do not give their own opinions about real-life issues. Instead they share God's truth. As the Creator of life and Author of relationships, He is the only Source of wisdom that counts.

So, when you are asked to give counsel, don't give your thoughts or opinion. Share God's Word and pray with the person who came to you. There is immeasurable wisdom in His Word and amazing power in the prayers of His chosen ones!

HIS PRINCESS IN ACTION

I am blessed to be surrounded by the wise men and women of God who serve on our ministry advisory board. I cannot imagine how lost I would be if I looked to man's opinion for guidance.

Also, because I speak to large groups of women, I am privileged to have women share some of the deepest secrets of their hearts. Many of them ask me for answers to some of life's most difficult questions, and even though I teach the Word, I don't have the Bible memorized. I know, however, that if I can't give them an answer from God's Word, I can take these women to His throne in prayer.

Oh, we women do love to tell one another what to do and how to do it, but very well-meaning, lovely women of God can still give us the wrong advice at a critical time in life. I remember writing my mother after not having been in relationship with her for years. (I told you that story in the previous chapter.) She rejected my letter, and I was devastated. At the time, Christians who loved me advised me to let my mom go and not pursue the relationship further. They did not want to see me hurt any more, so they gave me their opinion, not God's Word or will for my relationship with my mother.

When I read my Bible the night I received my mother's letter, God guided me to the account of Peter asking Jesus how many times we are to forgive others. Jesus replied, "Seventy times seven" (Matthew 18:22, NLT). Well, that number was a far cry from the one time I had pursued my mom. Then I thought about my King and how He kept on pursuing me even when I rejected Him. And I decided to listen to the counsel of God's Word rather than the opinion of Christians who cared for me. I am not saying we should continue to pursue someone who keeps rejecting us. The prodigal son's father did not pursue his son. He gave him his entire inheritance and let him go (Luke 15:11–13). That didn't mean the father didn't love his son. However, there *are* times to pursue someone, like Jesus explained in the parable about leaving the flock to go after the one lost sheep (Matthew 18:12). There are also times to hold back, like the prodigal's father did, and wait on God's timing for reconciliation. Lastly, there are those times when we must let go and move on, like Paul and Barnabas did when they parted ways. They just couldn't work out their disagreements. But even though they walked away from their relationship, God still used each of them to multiply His ministry through their lives separately, instead of together.

The Lord led me to pursue my mom, and as you know, the outcome was total restoration. Today my mom and I are closer than ever. But many times the Lord has led me to hold back, wait, and pray for people. I have also had to completely separate myself from some people in order to complete the call on my life. So, not all situations end in restoration. We have no control over the outcome, but we are still blessed in doing what God would want us to do and how to do it. God's ways are not our ways. He knows what we need to do when we don't, and following His counsel will always lead to abundant life. Remember, "If it is possible, as far as it depends on you, live at peace with everyone" (Romans 12:18, NIV). He knows there are those people and situations that seem impossible, but peace comes inside of us when we do what we can, according to His Word.

Take a moment to reflect on a time you either received wrong counsel from well-meaning friends or offered words of your own wisdom and unintentionally led someone down the wrong path. Whichever lesson you learned, remember that God's Word teaches the art of loving one another. Let's pray…

His Princess Prayer

Dear God,

Please forgive me for giving or receiving counsel from anything or anyone other than You. Open my spiritual eyes to the truth of Your Word and engrave on my heart and in my mind every word of Yours I read. When caring people offer advice, please show me by Your Holy Spirit the thoughts that are from You and the opinions that are from man. I commit this day to look to You and You alone for the answers to every question and challenge that life brings.

In Jesus' name I pray, amen.

Complete One Another

*Just as our bodies have many parts and each part has a separate function,
so it is with Christ's body. We are all parts of his one body,
and each of us has different work to do. And since we are all one body in Christ,
we belong to each other, and each of us needs all the others.*

ROMANS 12:4–5, NLT

Can you imagine purchasing a work of art that isn't finished? You wouldn't even notice the part that was complete; you'd be so distracted by the rough and ragged places. And you definitely wouldn't display the art if you took it home—but my guess is that you wouldn't even take it home. You would want it finished before you invested in it.

Sadly, this unlikely scenario paints too accurate a picture of many relationships in our church body. We go to church, but we don't do our part to complete the picture of what God created the church to be. Rather than being an active, contributing part of the body, we break down the body by either ignoring people's needs, criticizing those members who are trying to do their part, or complaining about those who don't.

I remember when my stepmother, Susie, first became a Christian. She read the Bible every day. She watched Christian television, she listened to Christian music, and she was passionate for her King. But when I asked her why she didn't attend a church, she said, "Why do I need one? I have my own relationship with the Lord." My reply was, "Maybe the church needs you." On that very day she found a church, that Sunday she started attending, and she became a strong pillar of faith for many members who were weaker in their faith.

We too easily forget that the church exists not only for what we can *get*; it also exists for what we can *give*. Many of us feel alone in our churches because we have never truly been a part of completing anything or anyone in it. If the church is ever going to be a work of Christian art that the world will admire, then each of us needs to do our part to complete the picture. We are not called to sit on the sidelines until our Lord's return. God commands us in His Word to use the gifts He's given us and to be involved in His body. He calls us to invest our time and talents in completing the church.

Remember Jonathan, King Saul's son? In many ways, Jonathan completed David. He stood by David in his darkest hours, and he reminded David of God's call on his life. Even though David was eventually crowned king, both David and Jonathan will be rewarded in heaven for serving God and His people. We are to follow their example. We are to serve; we are the church.

Our pastors are not the church; they are not supposed to do all the work of ministry all by themselves—or even all the work of ministry in God's power! We are to help them complete the work our King called us all as a body to do together.

Take a moment to ask the Lord what He wants you to do to help complete the work of art that is His church.

His Princess Prayer

Dear God,

I am ready to do whatever work You have called me to do in Your church. Show me where I will best fit in Your plan. I don't want to be anywhere You have not called me to be. So I ask You now to put in my heart a passion and specific purpose so that I may serve You and Your people, the church.

In Jesus' name I pray, amen.

As I mentioned in the section on Romans 12:4–5 (previous chapter), God has placed a gift inside of you. Maybe you are good with children, and you need to volunteer once a month to work in Sunday school or children's church. Maybe you decorate well and can help prepare rooms for church events. If you can sing, then join the choir. If you love to host people in your home, open it up for a small group. You don't have to burn yourself out for the church. But if every single one of us contributed a little time and effort, then no one would be overwhelmed, and we—as individuals and as the church—would grow, and the work of the church would be complete. Our God says the harvest is great but the workers are few. Let's be the chosen few that invest in eternity for our King!

As our chapter on royal relationships nears its end, I encourage you to keep in mind that just as art has its many expressions, not all relationships look alike. Each person God has placed in our path is there for a different purpose and perhaps for a different season. No one person can provide all that we need and want from a relationship, and we need to let that be okay.

↬ If you have a girlfriend whom you truly connect with but your kids don't, then enjoy that friendship for what it is. Make time to be alone together without your kids.

↬ If you have a prayer partner who faithfully lifts you before God's throne but who doesn't desire to be in a social setting with you, value that relationship as the spiritual blessing that it is.

Too many times we walk away from a God-ordained relationship because all the pieces of that friendship don't fall into place the way we want or expected them to. But if we choose to enjoy each individual for who she is and for what we share when we're together, then we will greatly appreciate the value of our friendships.

Maybe you, like me, have many different kinds of relationships in your life. I have young girls who are daughters of my heart. I have older women who share their godly wisdom with me. I have friends who are great fun to play with. I have accountability partners and prayer partners, people who are very precious to me even though we are not together socially.

Think about the different people in your life and the place in your heart each one has. I pray that you will learn to love each of them differently and to value them for who they are and who you are when you are with them. The beauty of being in a variety of relationships is being able to express different sides of ourselves. Let's pray...

His Princess Prayer

Dear God,

Thank You for my friends. Help me not to pressure them to meet my every need and desire. Forgive me for looking to anyone other than You to satisfy my needs and wants. As I think about the people You've put in my path, help me to enjoy our differences and show me how I can learn and grow from each person. Also, Lord, fill me up so I can be a river of blessing that nourishes and refreshes others.

I pray this in Jesus' name, amen.

four

My Prince Will Come

GETTING READY FOR
MY LORD'S RETURN

ur Prince is coming to rescue us from the troubles of this world...and our story is *not* a Disney dream. It is the greatest love story ever told, and it's true. Our Prince loves us so passionately that He gave his life so we can and will live happily ever after. This final chapter is about getting ready for that glorious day when we finally see Him face-to-face on our wedding day in heaven. Even now, while you are reading, your Prince is preparing a place just for you.

GET A LOVE LIFE

*"No eye has seen, no ear has heard, no mind has conceived
what God has prepared for those who love him."*

1 CORINTHIANS 2:9, NIV

Our Lord knows how hard it is for us to keep our eyes on something we can't yet see. But it is possible. In fact, you've probably even done it before.

Do you remember back when you were a girl, dreaming about what true love would feel like? You and I had hope in our hearts that we would find that one person who would truly love us for who we are. Even though we could not see his face, we had our hopes and dreams to hold on to.

Now we are women, and many of us have yet to find true love. We don't feel rescued. We feel discouraged, and our dreams have turned into disappointment. Our hearts are no longer filled with hope of "happily ever after" but with the heaviness of heartache and hurt. Our Prince, however, longs to give us back our hopes and dreams for the future. Our hearts are safe with Him. He will never leave you or forsake you. He is longing to refresh our souls and love us back to life again. So let go of that little girl inside of you that needs to be loved, and let yourself fall in love with the Prince that loved you with His life.

His Princess Love Letter

My princess, My bride-to-be,

I love you beyond description. No words can describe how much I love you. I know sometimes you don't feel you deserve to be loved, but let Me remind you that you don't have to earn My love or affection. I stretched out My arms of love and died on the cross for you, My princess, so that you would know how passionately I love you and how priceless you are to Me.

Oh, dear precious one, I see your heartache. I know those who have broken your heart. Bring Me the pieces that remain after all the human hurts you've experienced, and I will show you how I—and I alone—can restore your soul. Don't look to anyone but Me, My love. No one understands you like I do.

I am the Lover of your soul. I'm the only One who can love you the way you long to be loved. I know you can't see Me, but My Spirit is within you. You can hear Me speak to you through My Word. You can enter into My presence anytime you wish. I'm only a prayer away. You will feel Me comfort you when you cry out to Me; you will experience My joy when you sing praises to Me. I am with you wherever you are. So hold on to hope, My beloved. I'm coming soon, and we will live happily ever after throughout eternity.

Love,

Your Prince and Savior who has loved you with His life

The greatest thing about letting yourself fall in love with your Prince is that He will never, ever reject you. The truth is, the more you allow yourself to love Him, the more you will feel His Holy and loving presence around you and within you. Let's pray...

His Princess Prayer

Lord,

Deliver me into Your arms of love. I'm ready to fall in love with You—and You alone—with all that I am. Break down the wall I have built around my heart and heal me from the wounds and scars left by those who have hurt me. I need to know You are really with me. Reveal Yourself in a very real way, Jesus. I want to believe I am Yours now and forever throughout eternity.

In Your precious name I pray, amen!

May you be able to feel and understand, as all God's children should,
how long, how wide, how deep, and how high his love really is;
and to experience this love for yourselves.

EPHESIANS 3:18, TLB

GET REAL WITH YOUR PRINCE

I pour out my complaints before him
and tell him all my troubles.
For I am overwhelmed,
and you alone know the way I should turn.

PSALM 142:2–3, NLT

Even though we have yet to meet our Prince face-to-face, He knows everything about us. Nothing is hidden from Him. He is waiting to have a very authentic and deep relationship with His bride-to-be.

We have a beautiful example in the Psalms of what a real relationship is like with the Lord. Our beloved King David is called "a man after [God's] own heart" (1 Samuel 13:14, AMP). There was nothing artificial about David's relationship with the Lord. If you read any of his psalms, you will see that David was extremely honest with his God. He didn't hide his rage, his fears, his disappointments, his worries, his praise, or his love from his heavenly Father. If you have not experienced that same closeness with Him, it may be because you have never known how to let yourself be entirely honest with Him. You can and will experience the intimacy you long for if you will take a chance and trade a mechanical religious relationship for a totally transparent and real relationship with the One who gave His life to save you—the One you will be spending all of eternity with.

Earlier we talked about how David overcame the temptation to kill King Saul when he had the chance. What we did not talk about is the very "real" and heartfelt prayer he cried out to God. It's found in Psalm 109:8, and you'll see there that David boldly asked that Saul's days be few and that God would replace him with a different king. This was David's eloquent way of saying, "Please let Saul go away somewhere in the wilderness and die!"

I remember when I fell out of love with my husband. I somehow thought that if I didn't talk to God in prayer about Steve, then He would not see what a failure I was as a wife. After several months of hiding my real feelings from the Lord, I finally made a list of all the things I resented Steve for. Then I dropped to my knees and got extremely honest and vulnerable with my Lord. *If King David poured out his complaints,* I thought, *why shouldn't I? I love the same God he loved.* I spent an hour crying and complaining.

When I finished pouring my heart out to my Lord with my "nasty list," I made a deal with Him. I took Him at His word and put His promise to the test…that He would never give me more than I could handle. So I confessed to Him that I could not handle staying in ministry when I didn't love my husband. I got open with God and gave Him a time frame for changing my heart toward my husband— or, I told Him, I would leave both Steve and the ministry.

To my complete surprise, within twenty-four hours of praying that prayer, I fell completely back in love with my husband. I was in the kitchen when I looked into Steve's eyes and began to cry uncontrollably. He said, "What's wrong?" I said, "I love you all over again." I realized at that moment that God keeps His promises. He was the only one who could rescue me from my despair and change my heart from hard and hopeless to ripe with love and right with Him.

I also realized that by holding onto my hurts and resentment rather than crying out to my King, I had allowed a spiritual cancer to enter my heart. It was killing me on the inside and spreading to other areas of my life.

Today I know the joy and freedom that come from having a truly authentic relationship with the God who gave me life. I have also learned to be honest with myself about the fact that I can't handle the trials, pain, or problems this life brings without constantly being in open and honest communication with my King. His love is truly amazing, and you and I are so blessed to be the bride of a Prince who provides peace, power, and protection for us. He is our safe place; after all, we are His princesses! He must long for us to run into His arms of unconditional love and tell Him anything and everything that is on our hearts. It's wonderful to know that His love for you and for me will never change, no matter what we feel or what we say to Him.

So don't listen when the enemy of your soul suggests that you can save yourself from the pain and problems of this world. When something hurts you or someone angers you, tell your Savior all about it. You don't have to wait for your Lord's return to begin to experience intimacy with Him! He is with you now in spirit, so cry out to Him about whatever is on your heart. Don't waste another moment walking alone. Your Prince is waiting for you to speak to Him, so open your heart and let Him love you and bless you with a peace that surpasses all human understanding.

HIS PRINCESS LOVE LETTER

My princess,

Don't be afraid to be your real self with Me. I know everything about you already, My love. I know how many hairs are on your head. I know when you lie down and when you are awake. I am your Prince, and I gave up My life so that you might have complete access to the throne room of heaven. It breaks My heart to see you in need and not coming to Me. I can and will meet your every need if you will allow Me into your life. I promise to always be your safe place and your Prince of Peace.

So come to Me now in truth. There is nothing you can tell Me that will change the way I feel about you. I love when you come to Me and share your feelings, your failings, and your fears. I can more fully reveal My power to you when you come to Me in complete honesty. I also want you to know how passionately I love you, but I will not ever force your honesty. So I wait patiently until you are ready.

Love, your Prince, who is everything you are searching for

*For I know the one in whom I trust, and I am sure that he is able
to safely guard all that I have given him until the day of his return.*

2 TIMOTHY 1:12, TLB

We can trust our Prince with our every deep, dark secret
and our every concern. So give yourself the greatest gift of
all, an intimate relationship with the One who gave His all
for you.

GET INTO HIS WORD

Basic Instructions Before Leaving Earth

*"Yes, I am the vine; you are the branches.
Those who remain in me, and I in them, will produce much fruit.
For apart from me you can do nothing."*

JOHN 15:5, NLT

One vital way to get closer to God is to read His Word. To
"remain in Him" is to read and study and meditate and
memorize and know His Word. Can you imagine receiving
love letters from your husband every day, yet refusing to
read them? You would never know the true expression of
his heart. You would not know how he thinks or what he
wants you to know. Your choice to ignore his letters would

make him feel terribly rejected, and you would be deprived of the intimacy with him that you long for. I'm sure our Lord feels the same way. He left us words of life, He expresses His love through those words, yet somehow we miss out on all we need to do and know to get ready for our glorious wedding day.

Why don't we long to read the written Word—"love letters" from our King?

I've discovered many reasons why. Let's look at one I know all too well.

I struggle to be still. Somehow I feel if I'm not running from the time I wake up until the time I drop into bed, I am not being productive. I feel like the bride who works frantically on the details of the wedding day but neglects the most important thing—my relationship with the One I'll be spending eternity with. When I live my days without the Word and don't make myself be still, I find myself exhausted and overwhelmed. Can you relate?

If you're struggling to make time to read God's Word, I encourage you to join a Bible study at your church or a home-group study. It really helps to have accountability partners like that. And I have discovered that the more I read God's Word, the more I desire to live for my King. When I am spending time reading the Bible, I think about my Prince all day long. Just as a love letter from my husband fills my heart with warmth and love, God's Word fills my spirit with His love and hope, and I feel His presence with me throughout my day. I've also discovered that the less I read God's written Word, the less I want to live for Him and the more I tend to live for myself—and that's not a good option for His princess. Let's pray...

His Princess Prayer

Dear Lord,

Forgive me for not spending more time reading the Bible and getting to know You better. Convict me when I make anything more important than spending time with You. Put in my heart a passion to be still, to sit at Your feet, and to listen to Your words of truth, Your declarations of love, and Your promises of faithfulness to me. Send a fresh wind of Your Spirit to clear away anything that keeps my heart from Yours, so that I will know You better and love You more.

In Jesus' name I pray, amen.

GET RIGHT WITH GOD

Yes, happy are those who delight in doing what he commands.
Their children will be successful everywhere;
an entire generation of godly people will be blessed.
PSALM 112:1–2, NLT

There is never a wrong time to get right with God. And one amazing thing about our relationship with Him is that we don't have to get right in order to go to Him. According to His Word, it is when we go to Him in confession that He makes us as clean as snow. Praise be to our God! But too many princesses think they have gone too far to ever turn back and get right with the King. That is a lie and the truth is this: God will always forgive us and remove our sins from us as far as the east is from the west. Also, God is passionate about helping us. He even turns the worst circumstances and greatest sins into something He can use for His kingdom.

King David—who loved God with all his heart and who, as a boy of great faith, stepped onto a battlefield with enough courage to confront and kill a giant—was the same king who shirked a duty. Instead of leading his mighty army into battle, David made the bad choice to stay home. That decision opened the door to temptation, and David walked right through—and he committed adultery with Bathsheba.

Then he tried to hide his sinful actions by putting Bathsheba's husband alone on the front line to ensure that he would be killed. Yes, we are talking murder and adultery from the man after God's own heart—and David was devastated by his own actions. When you read some of his psalms, you'll see that he expressed pain in a way that will tear at your heart. Even though he obviously felt the awfulness of his sin and far away from God, David knew that the only way to deal with his guilt and shame was to confess his sin to the One he had ultimately sinned against.

Now, confession of sin means forgiveness, but it doesn't mean that consequences of our actions will be negated. There are always consequences to our bad choices. But there is also redemption with our God. David had to live with the consequences of his choices, but—by God's grace and despite David's past sin—he went on to fulfill his royal call. God showed His neverending mercy in the blessed gift of King Solomon. And as we read earlier, this son of King David and Bathsheba became the wisest man who ever lived—the wisest king who ever ruled—even though his parents had sinned against God. Our Prince loves us with tenderness and mercy even when we do not deserve it. We are so blessed to belong to Him.

I thought I was totally free from the shame of my past until one day after I became pregnant with my first child.

On that afternoon the shame surfaced again—and quite powerfully.

My husband and I were so excited about going to the doctor to confirm that yes, we were going to have a baby. There I was, lying on the doctor's table, when he asked me if I wanted to hear my baby's heartbeat. I said, "How is that possible? I'm only six weeks pregnant." I had been told— wrongly!—that babies don't have heartbeats until they are at least twenty weeks old.

The doctor put the stethoscope to my tummy, and for the very first time I heard the beat of my son's heart. I began to cry.... My husband thought I was crying tears of joy. However, the truth is that I was crying tears of pain and regret—even terror!

How could such a miraculous moment bring that reaction? Distant memories flooded my mind. I choked back my tears as I recalled an afternoon twelve years earlier. I was only sixteen at the time, but lying on that doctor's table suddenly made it feel as if it were yesterday. One stupid mistake with a guy, and I had found myself pregnant. The abortion doctor told me I was doing the right thing. "It's only been six weeks. It's not a baby. It doesn't even have a heartbeat," he assured me.

Now I was confronted for the first time with the hor- rifying truth about that long-ago decision—and I was too ashamed to tell my husband. For several more years I lived with such shame and fear that I was sure God would take my son in order to punish me. I didn't know how there was any way I could get right with God for something so wrong, something that had happened so long ago.

My Prince finally rescued me over Easter weekend in 1999. It was Good Friday night, and we were at church. A big wooden cross had been displayed in the sanctuary, and each of us was holding a big nail and a small piece of paper. Then the pastor told the story of Easter unlike I had ever heard it before. When he finished, he invited anyone who was holding onto past sin or shame to write it on the paper, walk forward, pick up a hammer, and nail it to the cross.

I thought, *Can my Lord really remove the guilty stains and wipe away my shame?* I sat there paralyzed by my fear of what people would think if I walked forward. Finally, I felt the Spirit of God whisper, *Give Me your past. Give Me your shame.* I got up and walked toward the cross. The moment I picked up that hammer and drove the nail through my confessed sin, I felt the Lord whisper in my spirit, *This is why I had to die for you—so I could take away all your guilt and shame.* At that moment He replaced my past pain with His peace.

After that night, I began to understand that confession is more than just something God requires, some kind of "have-to" that we must deal with. Confession is a gift from God by which He replaces the strongholds of our past sin and shame with blessings of forgiveness and freedom, healing and hope. Today I am free from the fear of God's punishment, not because of anything I can do in my own power, but because my Prince paid the price for my sin. I am forgiven!

If you are holding onto something, maybe it's time for you to look at the cross as more than a symbol of your Savior's death. When our Lord died and rose again, He broke forever the power of sin on our lives.

Right now, take a moment to invite the Lord to search your heart for any unresolved sin from your past that continues to torment you. Don't wait until the wedding day! You can experience cleansing and freedom from *this* day forward!

His Princess Prayer

Lord,

I can't help but look back on my life with guilt and regret. I think about the things that I shouldn't have done or said and all the things that I could have done. I reflect on the times that I brought shame to You and myself, and pain to others. I know that Your Word says You have washed me white as snow and that You want me to let go of my guilt over what has gone wrong. But I can't do it without Your help. Please renew my mind with Your Word and help me to accept that You died for all my mistakes and sins. Help me to believe that I can become a new person with a new start in You. I'm ready to be free from the guilt of my past, and move on to a life of victory and purpose in You.

In Jesus' name I pray.

Love, Your princess, who accepts Your cleansing

Therefore, if anyone is in Christ, he is a new creation;
the old has gone, the new has come!

2 C O R I N T H I A N S 5 : 1 7, N I V

GET PASSIONATE ABOUT YOUR CALL

"I know all the things you do, that you are neither hot nor cold.
I wish you were one or the other! But since you are like lukewarm water,
I will spit you out of my mouth!"

R E V E L A T I O N 3 : 1 5 – 1 6, N L T

Nothing is more refreshing than stepping into a cool stream on a hot summer day. But when we lived in Arizona, the afternoons were so hot that our swimming pool was anything but refreshing. And there is nothing good about a lukewarm swimming pool on a blistering hot day. You step in expecting refreshment, but you can hardly tell whether you're even in the water.

When our lives are lukewarm for Jesus, people can step in and out and never feel refreshed…or warmed…or anything at all. Nothing good about being with us…nothing bad, either. What a tragedy.

Without passion for our Prince and His return, our lives are meaningless—nothing more than momentary, fleeting worldly pleasure (Ecclesiastes 2:11). Passion is the wind in our sails, the fuel in our engine. Where and how far we go with our passion depends on how much we are willing to be led by our Lord.

What will we do with our passion? Will we let God fan that spark into flame with the wind of His Spirit, or will we allow our passion to be misdirected or snuffed out by the distractions of this world?

Passion without a God-ordained purpose can become self-destructive, or it can prove totally useless, resulting in nothing of eternal value. But passion for our Lord is unstoppable and incredibly powerful. Promise Keepers is a perfect example of well-directed passion.

My guess is that the fire inside these men started when women cried out to their Lord on behalf of their marriages and their homes. Our God answered these prayers through Coach McCartney, a man whose passion for stronger marriages led him to start Promise Keepers. What an amazing sight to see tens of thousands of men gather for the purpose of becoming great leaders in our nation and in our homes by living holy lives by loving their wives, and leading their children in the ways of the Lord. The world got a glimpse of the power of Promise Keepers when one million men stood on the steps of the nation's capitol in Washington DC to declare publicly their promises to God and their families.

Think, too, about Mel Gibson, the man who was once on the cover of *People* magazine and declared the sexiest man alive. This is the same movie star who said he was lonely and miserable before he got passionate about doing something for God. That passion compelled him to produce a movie about our Lord's death and resurrection. God gave him the faith to invest his own financial resources and the courage both to stand up against every adversary that came against him (and there were a lot!) and to risk losing it *all*—his fame, his influence in Hollywood, and millions of dollars. No one in the movie business thought *The Passion of the Christ* would succeed, but it is one of the most talked-about movies of all time. Mel Gibson walked in God's favor during this project. He didn't even have to pay for publicity—the media took care of that for him! And he made more money from that one movie than from all of his previous movies *combined.* What a great example—and what great proof of what God's power, combined with our passion, can accomplish to further His kingdom.

Passion can be fueled in our hearts in many different ways. It can be rooted in long-held dreams and unshakable goals. Sometimes it comes through a simple prayer to our Prince, asking Him to give us the flame we need to do our part. If you are bored with your life, I invite you to enter the action and, with a short prayer, ask Him to show you what

He wants you to do. It will be the first of many adventures with the King!

Passion can also be birthed by tragedy. Such passion burns deeply within and is not easily blown out. Mothers Against Drunk Driving, for instance, was started by a mother whose child was killed by a drunk driver. When 9/11 hit our nation, we were in shock, and it appeared that nothing good could come of such a tragic event. As painful as the memory of that day will always be, God has brought a lot of good out of it. Our nation was (and still is) united more than it has been in decades. With all of us focused on the image of those burning towers, our differences did not divide us. Also, many people became passionate for God and began new—or renewed their—relationships with Him. We watched Christians throughout the world become passionate about praying for our nation and our president and more passionate about sharing the gospel with their neighbors. These are just two examples, but the list of great ministries and missions that started because of one compassionate tear or single broken heart is long, and each is a testimony of pain turned into purpose for eternity and a passion to do something great to further God's kingdom.

I have a younger brother who, like me, has made a lot of poor choices in his life. Also like me, he was devastated when our parents divorced and our family fell apart. Today he is a Christian, but—by his own choice—he lives in homeless shelters. I spent years wondering why such an intelligent man would choose the street over the comforts of a home.

Last year when I was in the Bay Area speaking at a conference, my husband and I took an afternoon off and drove to Santa Cruz, praying as we drove for God to allow us to minister to someone. It was too cold to walk on the beach, so we ventured into a coffeehouse on the pier to watch the sunset. We had just sat down when there, on the other side of the coffee bar, I saw a familiar face. It was my younger brother! Although we had kept in touch by phone, I had not seen him in person for years, and I barely recognized him. The hard life he had been living showed on his face, but his youthful exuberance still glimmered ever so faintly in the twinkle of his eye. Amazed that God had orchestrated such a divine appointment, I threw my arms around my brother.

Steve and I took Michael to dinner that night. It took everything in me to hold back the tears. One part of me felt angry with God for allowing our family to be so torn apart, and the other part of me was angry with my brother for not making something of his life. I hardly knew him anymore, but I still wanted a miracle for him. In fact, I wanted to rescue him from this life on the streets. I knew, however, that all the money in the world would not motivate him to become responsible.

After dinner Michael asked us to go to the apartment he was living in. When we got there, I saw that the place was more a commune of one-bedroom shacks than apartments. There were no families. Just prostitutes and drug dealers—and police officers patrolling every street. I was nervous about getting out of the car, but I could not refuse my brother's invitation to come in and meet his three roommates. There was little room for furniture, except for the two mattresses on the floor in the front room and two in the tiny bedroom.

"Your brother prays for us and teaches us about the Bible," one of the young girls told us. She had been a prostitute for several years—her young smile was hardened by years of pain and abuse. The second roommate wore heavy makeup and hardly spoke a word. My brother told us how he had been ministering to this young man—yes, man—since finding him on the streets. The other roommate was doing laundry in the sink and telling us how the three of them felt protected by my brother because of his love for Jesus.

As we hugged my brother good-bye, gave him some money, and promised him our prayers, we felt heartbroken for those people living in these conditions. Steve and I cried most of the drive back to the hotel, and we both felt ashamed for judging my brother. We had seen his passion for those who are homeless and hopeless. That day my anger turned into gratitude. I realized that even though Michael and I came from a broken home and chose completely different paths in life, we were both in full-time ministry and furthering God's kingdom. Michael was ministering to people on the streets, and I ministered to the women who are raising the next generation for God. Both of us are passionate for our call, in part because of the pain we experienced in our past. So don't let the pain from the past or poor choices you've made paralyze you any longer. Instead, let God use your pain to make you passionate. Whatever your prince has rescued you from, share the keys to that freedom with those who are still imprisoned in pain. You have the power inside of you to help them. God does not pull us out of the darkness to keep His light hidden inside of us. It is time to help those who are in our reach.

Keep in mind you do not have to go through great pain to have passion for your purpose. Passion is a prayer away. God also uses our hopes and dreams to make us passionate. So look inside yourself. What drives you? What do you care deeply about? Now take that dream before your King and ask Him to do something great through you for His eternal kingdom. If you have lost your passion for life, ask the Lord to restore it inside of you. Actually, let me pray for you right now.

His Princess Prayer

Dear Lord,

I lift this princess before Your throne. I ask You to restore in her the dreams she once held and the passion to do great things for You. Remind her that You can and will use her, whatever her past and whatever her present. Holy Spirit, I ask You to comfort, encourage, and restore in my sister a passion for You and for becoming a part of furthering Your kingdom. Give her now the desire of her heart, and let that desire burn passionately for You.

In Jesus' name I pray for her, amen.

GET A PRAYER LIFE WITH A PURPOSE

Pray at all times and on every occasion in the power of the Holy Spirit. Stay alert and be persistent in your prayers for all Christians everywhere.

EPHESIANS 6:18, NLT

I know from personal experience how hard it can be to believe that the God of the entire universe hears our prayers. I also used to think that there must be some magic formula I needed in order to make God's hand move when I asked. But today I know that we who name Jesus "Savior" really are royalty, that God really does hear our prayers, and that we have "anytime" access to the throne room of our King. When we begin to pray about everything, and especially when we pray with purpose, supernatural things happen. When we ask for God to do great things to further His kingdom, He always makes something great happen.

Yes, ask anything in my name, and I will do it!
JOHN 14:14, NLT

Our Prince loves our prayers, but His response may not be exactly what we asked for. It will most likely be better!

When I first became a mother, I wanted my son to see for himself the hand of God move in his life. So I began to pray with him when he was two, and almost every day Jake and I kept our appointment with God. We would ask Him to use us to do His work that day, and I was so encouraged to see a little boy be so passionate for prayer.

When Jake turned thirteen, I prayed that God would help him understand the true joy of giving. As I've mentioned, we live in a small town in Central Oregon where there is no mall. One day Jake and I drove to Portland for a big shopping spree. We had saved our money all year for our big day at the mall. As I drove, I prayed with Jake for a divine appointment—and our God didn't waste any time answering that prayer.

We walked into the mall and Jake was immediately off to the computer store. As I followed behind him, I happened to notice a young girl curled up on a bench, shaking. It was freezing outside and she did not appear to have a coat. I couldn't see her face but I could tell that she was in physical and emotional pain. My heart broke for her even before we spoke. I couldn't help myself…I wanted to do something to help, so I approached her and said, "Please let me pray for you." To my surprise she totally mocked me by responding sarcastically, "*Whatever*"—to which I shot back, "I'm not leaving until I pray for you." She looked at me with anger in her eyes and said, "Go ahead and get it over with." Jake walked up to us just as I began to pray this prayer:

Dear God,

I don't know what this girl has been through, but You do, so please let her know You love her and that You can and will help her. Please show her today, somehow, that You see her broken heart and You can restore all she has lost.

In Jesus' name I pray, amen.

This precious girl went from cold and distant to crying uncontrollably, and she began to share her story through her tears. She had gotten pregnant, but her parents had wanted her to abort the baby. She wanted to keep the baby and marry her boyfriend, who was the father of the child. Her parents had kicked her out on the streets. She and her boyfriend kept the baby, slept under a bridge, and still went to high school. But because they were homeless, they had given the baby up for adoption.

The girl's boyfriend walked up while she was sharing their story, and my son said out loud, "Mom, it's time to shop." I said, "Jake, did you hear their situation?" He said, "Yes, that's why we need to spend our shopping money on them." That day Jake took the young man and bought him clothes, a sleeping bag, new shoes, and a backpack. I took the young girl and did the same. At the end of our time with them, we got to pray the greatest prayer of all—the prayer for salvation. Then our ministry cut a check to get them in an apartment and off the streets.

As Jake and I drove back home without any shopping bags in our car, Jake said to me, "Mom, that was the best day I have ever had!" At that moment I realized that Jake will never remember anything I bought him when he is old, but he will never forget the day God used his life as a gift to someone else. We don't need money to build those kinds of priceless memories with our children. If anything, money distracts us from what is really valuable in this life... and *acting according to our divine purpose, living in God's power, and seeing Him answer our prayers* are three of life's greatest treasures. Those are not things we can buy for our children. They are part of a legacy we build inside of them by our own examples of praying with purpose and acting on God's leading.

One more thing... I have discovered that when my family most needs God, we are so much closer. Those hard times drive us to our knees to pray together.

You and I need to pass on to our children the great gift of a prayer life with purpose!

Now glory be to God who...is able to do far more than we would ever dare to ask or even dream of—infinitely beyond our highest prayers, desires, thoughts, or hopes.

EPHESIANS 3:20–21, TLB

His Princess Prayer

Dear God,

    I want to pray with purpose. Help me to know that You hear me when I call to You—and give me the courage to ask You to do great things. Remind me that it is my privilege to come to You in all things—and thank You that You care enough to listen to my every request.

    In Jesus' name I pray, amen.

GET FAITH

What is faith? It is the confident assurance that what we hope for is going to happen. It is the evidence of things we cannot yet see.

HEBREWS 11:1, NLT

Our Prince knows how hard it can be for us to believe in something we cannot yet see. It can become very hard to stay focused on Him when our personal world seems to be falling apart and our foundation is shaken by circumstance.

But if we are His bride-to-be and we're going to live by faith, we will have to take Him at His word and trust Him in all things. His Word says this about faith:

Without faith it is impossible to please God.

I don't know about you, but I've sure felt like the disciples must have felt as they clung to their boat out on the stormy seas. When storms have hit my life, I've wondered—as I'm guessing those disciples did—*Is my Lord sleeping while I'm drowning in my troubles and my worries? Is He going to rescue me from this fear, or will it overtake me?* But then I think about Jesus asking Peter to walk out on the water. Peter didn't begin to sink until he took his eyes off his Lord and focused on his circumstances, some what-ifs, and the very real possibility that he could drown (Matthew 14:30). The disciples—especially Peter—teach us the secret to true faith…and that is to keep our eyes locked on our Lord, not on our lives.

Here are some of the things we can do to keep our eyes steadily on our Prince:

1. We can turn fear into faith by choosing to pray instead of worry.

2. We can go immediately to His Word and remind ourselves of who He is and review His promises.

3. We can play praise music throughout our day to stay
   focused on Him.

4. We can call a friend to pray for us, especially when we
   feel too weak to pray for ourselves.

5. We can write down a specific promise from His Word
   regarding our situation and either memorize it or post
   it where we will see it often.

6. We can write prayers (our love letters to God) in a jour-
   nal. This is a physical act by which we hand the situation
   over to our Lord. And in the future, when we face new
   challenges, we will be able to look back and read about
   His faithfulness to us in the past.

No one will be able to stand up against you all the days of your life.
As I was with Moses, so I will be with you;
I will never leave you nor forsake you.

JOSHUA 1:5, NIV

What an awesome promise from our Prince!

He longs for us to truly trust Him and to take Him at
His Word. Many times our faith in Him grows during life's
most difficult and challenging circumstances. For instance,

can you imagine what kind of faith it must have taken Mary, the mother of Jesus? Think about it.... Imagine a sixteen-year-old virgin being told by an angel that she was pregnant by the Holy Spirit and that she would deliver the Son of God, the Savior of the world. What would her fiancé think—and do? But she trusted God and His plan for her life.

And then there's Noah. Today his story is famous because of the faith he had. But when he was building an ark, there was not a sign of rain in the sky. I'm sure that his neighbors mocked him, and his wife, sons, and daughters-in-law certainly asked him many times, "Are you sure God is really going to flood the earth?" Yet Noah's family followed his leadership because of their faith in God, and we all know how the story ends.

And remember Sarah? When God first promised her a baby, she had faith, but over time she got tired of waiting on the Lord and His timing. So she decided to help God's promise be fulfilled and had her husband sleep with a servant so she could have the baby she longed for. As her plan unfolded, though, Sarah found herself jealous, bitter, and miserable. But our gracious God still gave her Isaac, the baby son He had promised.

Now, I can relate a little bit to Sarah because I, too, always wanted a baby daughter. Oh, I adored my son, but my heart still longed for a little girl, and God promises to give us the desires of our heart (Psalm 37:4). He doesn't put those desires in our heart to torment us, but I miscarried three babies, and I so longed to be the mother of a little girl. After my third loss I asked the Lord to either give me a daughter or take the desire of my heart totally away. Well, God did not remove the desire. It actually became even more intense, but I didn't have enough faith to trust Him. So, when I was about to turn forty, I asked my husband to get a vasectomy. I thought that if it were physically impossible to have children anymore, then I would stop wanting another one. Like Sarah, I took matters into my own hands.

Six weeks after Steve's surgery, I was in Nashville for a Christian booksellers' convention. While I was there, an author whom I had just met at the convention walked up to me and said, "Is it your heart's desire to have a daughter?" I replied, "Yes, but it's too late for me." She said, "Actually, the Lord told me that you're pregnant now with that little girl you long for." Of course I didn't believe her, so the next morning she knocked on my hotel door with two pregnancy tests in her hands. (She knew it would take two for me to believe it!)

Overwhelmed by the news, I called Steve right away, and he responded by saying, "Don't tell anyone in case we lose this baby too." Fear immediately stole my joy, and my faith was nowhere to be found. I knew that my dear husband was just trying to protect me from greater heartbreak, but I wanted to tell *everyone*! Praise God that the Spirit of our Lord rose up inside of Steve. He immediately ran back into the hotel room and said boldly, "Tell everyone you can to pray so we can have our girl!" We were at the right place to ask for prayer because this trade show draws about six thousand Christians. Then later, while I was being interviewed, I shared the news of my pregnancy—and the program host asked all the listeners nationwide to pray for our precious girl! I praise God for that prayer covering, because we welcomed our baby girl into the family on October 23, 1999. Even though I got in God's way, He gave me the desire of my heart.

In light of my own experience, I want to encourage you to ask God to either give you the desire of your heart or change your heart in accordance with His perfect will. I met an older woman who never did get the daughter she so desired. Instead she gave birth to three sons. However, when those boys grew up and got married, they became wonderful Christian husbands and they each had three daughters. God didn't give this praying woman the one daughter she wanted, but He did give her nine granddaughters—and she loves every minute she spends with them. But, she said, she also enjoys giving them back! Let's pray...

His Princess Prayer

Dear Jesus...my Prince of Peace,

Forgive me for not trusting You. Remind me that You are always faithful to keep Your promises. How could I doubt the One who gave His very life for me? Yet so often I do. Teach me to trust Your every word, remind me of Your great faithfulness to me, and help me never to stop believing that You always know what is best for me and that Your will is so much better than my way.

In Your name I pray, amen.

Your faithfulness extends to every generation, as enduring as the earth you created.

PSALM 119:90, NLT

GET ACCOUNTABILITY

The ear that hears the rebukes of life
will abide among the wise.
He who disdains instruction despises his own soul.
PROVERBS 15:31–32, NKJV

Proverbs warns that pride can actually destroy us. Pride comes before being destroyed and a proud spirit comes before a fall (Proverbs 16:18). Pride can be the very thing that keeps us from allowing someone to hold us accountable to living in a way that honors God. It takes humility to allow someone to see our weaknesses and then hold us accountable for dealing with them. But don't let your fear of what people will think about your weaknesses keep you from getting the accountability you need. Those people you are trying so hard to impress won't matter at all when you are answering to your King for your actions here on earth.

Too many of us, however, care more about our image than about living a righteous life that glorifies our King. We would rather keep secret sins stored in our souls and pretend that we are perfect than admit our weaknesses. Such attempts to hide never work out. Instead, those things we try to keep hidden can eventually come out in very destructive ways and even end up ruining our Christian witness. I write from experience, and I am so grateful that God put strong, faithful friends in my path as I headed toward destruction. These people were real friends; they weren't afraid to demand that I walk away from an emotional affair—and to hold me accountable to doing so. My sin would have resulted in the total devastation of my family, my ministry, and my witness for Christ. If you and I pridefully think we can't or won't fall, we are definitely setting ourselves up for failure.

One reason King David fell into sin with Bathsheba was because he wasn't where he was supposed to be. Furthermore, at that time, David didn't have someone to remind him about his duties as God's appointed and anointed King. Only later did David have the prophet Nathan confront him when he fell into sin, and God used that confrontation to get David back on the path of righteousness and help him stay committed to God's call on his life.

No matter how much you love your Lord, you can fall just as hard and far as King David did. We are not meant to walk the Christian walk alone. I used to think I could never fall because I am so passionate about my call to ministry. Well, I was wrong—as you read about earlier. Today I am surrounded by several accountability partners. I have eight wise and godly men and women on our ministry board who give me counsel. Someone else holds me accountable for my food issues, and another person helps keep me focused on my first and most important ministry… to my husband and my children.

Now I know it might appear like I'm some spiritual wimp with so many people helping me live out my faith, but I would rather look weak in the eyes of others and be able to finish strong for my King!

- ☞ QUEEN ESTHER had Mordecai to help her fulfill God's call on her life.
- ☞ MOSES had his brother Aaron to stand by him and, early on, even speak for him.
- ☞ KING DAVID had Jonathan to encourage him.
- ☞ MARY had Joseph standing by her while she was pregnant with the King of the world.

HIS PRINCESS WISDOM

The person whom you allow to know you so intimately will play a vital role in your life. But before you share your secrets with someone, I want to caution you to choose wisely and to look for the following characteristics in your possible candidates. Do not ask anyone to hold you accountable unless you can answer yes to all of the following questions about them!

1. Is the person's walk with God strong and consistent?
2. Does this person love you enough to be truthful with you?
3. Can you trust this person to keep your personal matters private?
4. Will this candidate take seriously the job of holding you accountable?
5. Do you feel comfortable being honest and transparent with this person?
6. Will this partner in the faith continually pray for you?
7. Will this person make time to call you or meet with you once a week to keep up with what you are doing?

Don't be discouraged if you can't think of a person who can hold you accountable. Instead, continue to pray and ask your Prince to provide the person He knows you need to fulfill your royal call. Remember that He wants you to stay close to Him and to be ready for His return. So you can know that if you ask, He will give you that perfect accountability partner in His perfect time. In the meantime, get yourself into a small group at your church.

His Princess Prayer

Dear Lord,

Please send me the perfect accountability, a person appointed and ordained by You. Enable me to be real with that person about my goals and dreams, my temptations and weaknesses, my sins and my fears. I trust that You will help me finish strong this journey of faith and find me the perfect fit for what I need to walk faithfully with You.

In Jesus' name I pray, amen.

GET AVAILABLE

There is a time for everything,
a season for every activity under heaven.
ECCLESIASTES 3:1, NLT

Many things have to be done to prepare for a wedding banquet, and we have to be careful to plan all the details in an orderly fashion. If we try to *be* everywhere at once and *do* everything at once, we will become overwhelmed and lose the joy of preparing for the big day. There's one thing our Prince does *not* require of us, and that's to be a frazzled, exhausted, burned-out bride!

First and foremost, you and I simply need to be available to our Prince, and that means "being still" so that we can hear Him speak to us. Ask God for the wisdom to know what He wants you to be available for during this season of your life.

Being available means being where you are most effective and most needed, whatever season of life you're in. Our ministry as the King's chosen bride happens wherever we are, wherever He has placed us. Remember that busyness does not equal success in our spiritual life. If anything, busyness can take away from everything we desire to be and rob us of time we need with our Lord, reading His Word and praying.

Busyness does not equal success

in our spiritual life.

HIS PRINCESS WISDOM

⊷ IF YOU ARE NEWLY MARRIED…being available to get to know your new husband is the best investment you can make in your marriage. Being married is very different from dating. Too many engaged couples make the mistake of thinking that the wedding is the goal of the relationship. This way of thinking sets them up for disappointment and the relationship up for failure. To know joy and success instead and in order to fulfill the very purpose of marriage— becoming one—we must study the needs and wants of our spouse. That is the ministry God wants you to devote yourself to. If anything interferes with your relationship with your husband (church activities, hobbies, exercising, goals, work, even family or friends), then you will need to consider your priorities and prayerfully decide what to invest your greatest energy and efforts in. Keep in mind that you just promised to share your life with that one special person…so share it!

⊸ IF YOU'RE A NEW MOM…it is your season to adjust to motherhood—and that means resting whenever you have the chance. The Word tells us that children are a gift from the Lord (Psalm 127:3, NLT), but they will seem more like a burden than a blessing if you are too busy and too tired. I mentioned earlier that God surprised me with my daughter when I turned forty. What I didn't share is that when I became pregnant, my speaking and writing ministry was thriving. I was speaking to over forty thousand women a year, my books were on the bestseller list, I was scheduled two years in advance for women's conferences, and I had just signed a five-book contract with Multnomah Publishers. It seemed like a strange time for God to finally answer my prayer for a baby. Why was I now entering back into the "baby season" all over again? I assumed this was the Lord's way of telling me that the ministry outside my home was coming to an end. So I cancelled everything I could in order to be available for Emily's arrival.

Now it had been years since I had been at home full-time. I felt a little lonely and depressed while I waited for her to come. Even though I wanted with my whole being to be a mother to my precious daughter, I had forgotten about all the sacrifices I would have to make for this new baby. But my heart completely changed after Emily was born and unable to breathe on her own for almost ten minutes! During those moments I realized that I was willing to give up *anything* just to see her live. She did live, and I settled into that baby season of life again. Now, five years later, God has resurrected my speaking and writing ministry, but I am careful to limit my outside ministry schedule to ensure that Jake and Emily know, without a doubt, that my ministry to them comes first.

⮎ IF YOU HAVE ELDERLY PARENTS TO CARE FOR…this is your season to be available to them. We honor God when we honor our parents by taking care of them. Someday when we are older, we may need our children to care for us. The choices we make about caring for our parents sets an example for our children. Also, the elderly are the wisest people on earth. They have had the hardest and longest education of all...*life itself!* So time with our parents can be precious tutorials for us as we give them the opportunity to share what they've learned. This generation is missing out on a wealth of wisdom by regarding our elders less and less.

↬ IF YOU ARE EXHAUSTED OR ILL...this is your season to rest and restore your health and spirit. Taking time to rest is not a reason to feel guilty. Guilt is not from God. But sickness and exhaustion can be His way of getting you to stop, be still, and take the time necessary to heal physically, emotionally, and even spiritually. I learned this lesson the hard way when I passed out while speaking in front of a very large audience. Needless to say, I hadn't heeded our Lord's warning to rest or to at least slow down...way down. We need to respect the limits of our body and mind. If our Lord asks us to lie down, then we need to lie down! If we don't, we could experience early death—and

I'm not necessarily referring to physical death. Exhaustion could mean the death of a ministry or the end of fruitful relationships.

✧ IF YOU ARE IN A CRISIS…it is a time for you to let go of any and all responsibilities that you can, to remove yourself from any and all commitments where you are not absolutely needed. "Life happens," and we need to be available where we are most needed. Our Prince will never give us more than we can handle, but we may take upon ourselves more than He would require of us. So when you are in crisis, ask your King what He wants you to do. During tough times, ask Him what He's trying to show you and say to you. Then write down all that He reveals to you in your spirit so that you will remember His words—and cling to Him.

I believe if the Lord wrote a letter to you about your availability, it might read like this:

His Princess Love Letter

My princess,

Give Me your plans. I know you have ideas in your mind about how everything should unfold in your life. You even have an agenda for this very day. But because I love you, I need you to give Me back all your plans for today— and for all your tomorrows. Remember, My love, that My ways are not your ways. If you will give Me a chance, I will show you how I want you to spend your days. I've ordained different seasons of life for different purposes. I know your heart longs to do many things. But if you will be available to Me, I will do more for you than you could ever do for yourself.

Love, your King who is always available to you

The steps of the godly are directed by the LORD.
He delights in every detail of their lives.
PSALM 37:23, NLT

GET AN ETERNAL VIEW

*So we don't look at the troubles we can see right now;
rather, we look forward to what we have not yet seen.
For the troubles we see will soon be over,
but the joys to come will last forever.*

2 CORINTHIANS 4:18, NLT

Our Prince will rescue us from the troubles of this world, but the fact is that this life can hit extremely hard at times. At those times the hope of heaven is the only thing we have to hold on to, and even though it may not feel like it, that is all we need. We will be able to make our mark for all eternity while we are here when we focus on the hope of the good things to come once we are finally home in His loving arms.

*We will never truly know that our God is all we need
until He is all we have to hold on to.*

We have all had times in our lives when we wonder how we will get through to the other side of the circumstances or the pain. Even our Prince cried out to His Father in heaven and said, "My God, my God, why have you forsaken me?" (Matthew 27:46). But He kept His eyes on His Father and on His Father's eternal purpose. If our Savior hadn't kept His eyes fixed on eternity, we would never get our "happily ever after." Thank You, Jesus! His death on the cross gives us hope for the future as well as hope for the present.

Now, I've been in ministry for several years, and many people's stories have made me wonder where God was in their pain and how they could have found any hope in the darkness. One particular story is engraved in my memory. I received a phone call from a nurse who was taking care of an AIDS patient named Cindy. The nurse said Cindy had been reading one of my books and wanted to talk to me about God before she died. Being passionate about any opportunity to lead someone to the Lord, I said, "Of course I'll call Cindy!"

But the nurse put something of a damper on my enthusiasm when she described in an e-mail the situation I was walking into. I won't go into detail about Cindy's life, but I will say that it was the worst story of abuse by men I have ever heard, and now she was going to die because of their sin. I found myself feeling very afraid to call Cindy. I told the Lord that I could not tell her He was a good God, and I felt paralyzed and unable to pray after hearing her excruciatingly painful story. So I asked others to pray for me.

After five days of fighting with God in my spirit and urgent messages and pleas from Cindy's nurse, I finally picked up the phone and dialed the hospital where she was. Cindy answered, and God gave me these words of eternal truth:

> Cindy, I know that men have done horrible things to you, and I know that many of them called themselves Christians. But they weren't acting like God's people! I beg you not to let those men keep you from going to a place where your heavenly Father will wipe away every tear you have ever cried. Ask Jesus into your heart and forgive those men, and I promise that you will be in a place where no one will ever hurt you again. You will be in the arms of the very God who died for you and who longs to spend eternity with you.

Cindy hung up on me, and I was devastated—until one week later when her nurse called me. She told me that Cindy had asked Jesus into her heart and had asked the nurse to tell me that she will see me in heaven.

- ⤷ It was an eternal view that gave me the courage to call Cindy and tell her about heaven.
- ⤷ It was an eternal view that gave Cindy the will to forgive those men and let her newfound Prince take her home.

We live in a fallen world, and tragically, innocent people suffer because of the sins of others. Pain is an inevitable part of this life, but as the King's chosen bride, we are not to take our eyes off eternity. We who are His chosen are the only ones who can share with this world the good news about Jesus and eternal life, the good news of the hope that we have in our King.

Our Prince is preparing our home in heaven, and no eye has seen, no ear has heard, and no mind has imagined the things He has prepared for those who love Him (1 Corinthians 2:9). We are definitely not home yet! And we all have people around us who need the Savior, so we need to fight the good fight as Paul did, and complete our royal call as Queen Esther did, until it is time for our Lord to rescue us.

Remember this truth: If we never receive one worldly blessing while we are here, we still have all we need and more because:

- We have eternal life.
- We have eternal hope.
- We have peace of mind and spirit.
- We have God's power inside of us.
- We have a home waiting for us in heaven.
- We have a real Prince who is coming soon.

↝ We will live happily ever after when this life is over.

We do not know the time or date of our wedding with the Prince. But we do know He is coming, and He wants us to be ready for His return.

My prayer for you as we close our time together is this:

His Princess Prayer

My dear princess,

May you never again doubt how much you are loved by your Prince and how important you are in our King's eternal plan. I also pray that our Prince will put a passion in your soul so intense that you will have the courage to take your royal position and possess a deep conviction to live boldly as the princess you are destined to be.

In Jesus' name I lift you up and pray, amen.

His Princess Love Letter

My Princess...You Begin and End with Me

You need not worry when your life will end, My precious child. All you need to know is that your first breath began with Me, and your last breath will lead you to My presence. Don't ever let fear of death or eternity frighten you. Your todays and tomorrows are secure with Me—I have held them in My hand since before you were born. When you finish your brief time on earth and I call you into My presence, your forever life in heaven will begin. But for now, My chosen one, you must live free from fear. Instead, trust Me to take you through every trial that comes your way. Remember that nothing in the universe can separate us. I am with you always...even until the end of time. So live well and finish strong— fixing your hope on the day that we will meet face-to-face on the other side of eternity.

Love, your eternal King

If I never meet you in this life, know that I look forward to celebrating with you throughout eternity. Until then, let's prepare ourselves for His glorious return!

Love,

Your sister princess in Christ,

Sheri Rose Shepherd

Let us be glad and rejoice and honor him.
For the time has come for
the wedding feast of the Lamb,
and his bride has prepared herself.

REVELATION 19:7, NLT

About the Author

Sheri Rose Shepherd has been a motivational speaker and Bible teacher for fifteen years as well as the keynote speaker for the Women of Virtue conferences and the national spokesperson for Teen Challenge ('94–'98). Sheri Rose has the gift to give all generations an eternal view of their lives. She shares with total transparency how God carried her from a dysfunctional, Jewish, "Hollywood" home and a life of drugs, depression, and an eating disorder to become a daughter of the King. Her speaking style is humorous, heartwarming, and based on biblical truth.

This former Mrs. United States does not talk of worldly accomplishments; rather, she shares about the crown of life. She takes us back to the truth about who we are, how much we are loved, and why we are here. In spite of battling dyslexia, she has written several books including *Life Is Not a Dress Rehearsal*.

Her life story has been featured in national magazines and on television shows like *Inside Edition* and *Lifetime Television for Women*. Her message about becoming His princess is scheduled to air on an upcoming Focus on the Family broadcast.

To schedule Sheri Rose to speak at your next event or for a free sample of her teaching, please call His Princess Ministries office at 541/410-0304 or 615/370-4700.

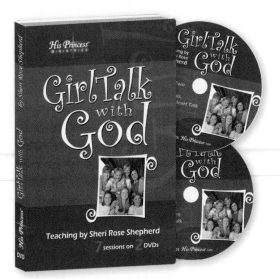

His Princess™
M I N I S T R I E S

We would love to hear from you!

If you would like to contact Sheri Rose, schedule her to speak at your next event, or request information on His Princess™ conferences, please visit www.HisPrincess.com.

Note for women's ministry directors and pastors' wives: Please call (602) 407-8789 to receive a free sample teaching on CD or tape.

You Are God's Masterpiece

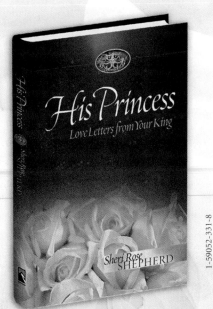

Give yourself the gift of hearing His voice speak directly to you in these beautiful scriptural love letters from your King. Let your soul soak in His love as each letter reminds you WHO you are, WHY you are here, and HOW much you are loved.

I have many devotional books, but very few have found their way into my morning quiet-time ritual. But from the first day I began His Princess I knew this was a book I wanted to read every day. Encouraging and insightful, this book reminds me how special I am to my Lord. I love this book!

—Tricia Goyer, amazon.com reviewer

The King Is Awaiting Your Presence!

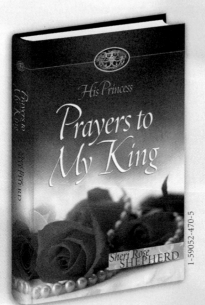

Prayers to My King is a beautiful gift book created to help women connect intimately with their God. While the first book in the His Princess™ series reminded us that we are loved intimately and unconditionally by our King, this second book helps us express our deepest thoughts, desires, fears, and failures by crying out to God through prayer.